BIBLICAL PRINCIPLES OF FINANCE:

The Cure for Financial Depression

Clyde L. Posey

WestBow
PRESS

WestBow Press™
1663 Liberty Drive
Bloomington, IN 47403
www.westbowpress.com
Phone: 1-866-928-1240

First published by WestBow Press: 08/10/2010

ISBN: 978-1-4497-0026-3 (sc)
ISBN: 978-1-4497-0027-0 (dj)
ISBN: 978-1-4497-0025-6 (e)

Library of Congress Control Number: 2010934553

Printed in the United States of America

This book is printed on acid-free paper.

Bible References Used

AMP—The Amplified Bible, Scripture taken from THE AMPLIFIED BIBLE, Old Testament copyright © 1965, 1987 by the Zondervan Corporation. The Amplified New Testament copyright © 1958, 1987 by the Lockman Foundation. Used by permission.

ESV—English Standard Version, "Scripture quotations are from The Holy Bible, English Standard Version® (ESV®), copyright © 2001 by Crossway Bibles, a publishing ministry of Good News Publishers. Used by permission. All rights reserved."

KJV—King James Version, 1994 (Originally 1611)

LB—Living Bible [paraphrased], 1971

NASB—New American Standard Bible, 1971

NCV—The Holy Bible-New Century Version, Scripture quoted from *The Holy Bible, New Century Version®* copyright © 1987, 1988, 1991 by Word Publishing, a division of Thomas Nelson, Inc. Used by permission.

NET—SCRIPTURE QUOTED BY PERMISSION. QUOTATIONS DESIGNATED (NET) ARE FROM THE NET BIBLE® COPYRIGHT © 2005 BY BIBLICAL STUDIES PRESS, L.L.C., www.bible.org ALL RIGHTS RESERVED.

NIV—New International Version, Scripture taken from the HOLY BIBLE, NEW INTERNATIONAL VERSION ®, Copyright © 1973, 1978, 1984 by International Bible Society. Used by permission of Zondervan. All rights reserved.

NKJV—New King James Version, 1991

NLT—Holy Bible-New Living Translation, Scripture quotations are taken from the *Holy Bible*, New Living Translation, copyright © 1996. Used by permission of Tyndale House Publishers Inc., Wheaton Illinois 60189. All rights reserved.

REB—Revised English Bible, 1989

RSV—Revised Standard Bible, Old Testament, 1952; New Testament, 1946

TCR—Thompson Chain Reference Bible, Scripture taken from the New King James Version, Copyright ©1982 by Thomas Nelson, Inc. Used by permission. All rights reserved.

TM—The Message [Eugene H. Peterson's paraphrase], Scripture taken from *THE MESSAGE* Copyright © 1993, 1994, 1995, 2000, 2001, 2002. Used by permission of NavPress Publishing Group.

TABLE OF CONTENTS

PREFACE

The Authority and Authenticity of Scripture

Without apology, this entire book is based on the authority and authenticity of "The Holy Bible." In the original Hebrew, Aramaic, and Greek texts, God's Word is inerrant, inspired, and *totally without any blemish of any kind.* In the New International Version of the Bible, II Timothy 3:16-17 is translated:

All Scripture is God-breathed and is useful for teaching, rebuking, correcting, and training in righteousness, so that the man of God may be thoroughly equipped for every good work.

The Greek word which is translated as "God-breathed" is *"theopneustos."* Theopneustos literally means the breath of God. Scripture is the very essence of Almighty God.

As a former Faculty Sponsor of the Collegiate Ministry of Navigators at Fresno State University (CSUF), I am familiar with testimony of Leroy Eims, former full-time minister of The Navigators. When Leroy was asked whether he believed the Bible from cover-to-cover, he replied essentially, "No, I believe the cover also. It says The Holy Bible." That is the same position that I take with regard to the Word of God. It is totally true and without error in the original manuscripts.

Those truths of God provide the foundation for this work. It is my prayer that God's Holy Spirit will lead, guide, and direct you as you read this book. *As you do, may God bless you in accordance with III John 2 (KJV):*

"Beloved, I wish above all things that thou mayest prosper And be in health, even as thy soul prospereth."

Other Factors

While the primary emphasis on this work is for U. S. citizens, it will have application for citizens of other countries as well. However, non-U.S. readers should generally disregard references which are specific to the U.S.A.

CAVEATS CONCERNING TAX ADVICE AND INVESTMENT COUNSELING

This book is not intended to provide *specific* tax advice or investment counseling. Where tax considerations are discussed, the reader should confirm that those provisions are still applicable and have not been changed by Congress, the Department of Treasury interpretation, or judicial decisions. It is generally best to obtain tax advice which is specifically related to your unique situation. The information provided here is conceptual and may not be applicable to your specific situation.

Additionally, the only guarantee concerning investment counseling is that all investments will perform in one of three possibilities. They will either: (1) go down, (2) go up, or (3) remain the same. Investments should be made in accordance with your specific investment goals, your risk tolerances, and your peace of mind. Every person's precise financial condition is unique and any investment should be made only after appropriate investigation has been made for all reasonable alternatives. This book is an inadequate substitute for a thorough evaluation of your specific investment situation.

CHAPTER 1

RATE OF RETURN ON INVESTMENT: *"THE PERFECT INVESTMENT"*

"For what shall it profit a man, if he shall gain the whole world, and lose his own soul?" **Mark 8:36 (KJV)**

"What good is it for a man to gain the whole world, yet forfeit his soul?" **Mark 8:36 (NIV)**

"What good would it do to get everything you want and lose you, the real you? What could you ever trade your soul for?" **Mark 8:36 (TM)**

What is the relationship between loss of a soul and "rate of return on investment"? If you lose your soul; you have lost everything in this world and the kingdom to come. Loss of soul nullifies all worldly investment returns because an eternity spent in hell will not compensate a person for any amount of monetary return earned on this earth.

"Rate of Return on Investment" (hereafter: rate-of-return) is the term that is used by an investor to measure the percentage returns on an investment for a specified level of risk. For example, if a person were to invest $100 in a $5 preferred stock, the rate of return could be computed by dividing the return by the cost in the following manner:

rate-of-return = average return/cost = $5/$100 = 5% per annum

This computation can be used to evaluate alternative investments with comparable risk. Most investors attempt to maximize the rate of return for a specified level of risk. While this book has been designed primarily for Christians; there may be readers who have not accepted Jesus Christ as their Savior at this point in their lives. Therefore, I would like to direct the reader to benefits available to the Christian from a financial point-of-view.

While rate-of-return is not the usual way of analyzing salvation, accepting Jesus as one's Savior has immeasurable benefits and returns. From a rate-of-return analysis, absolutely nothing provides a greater rate-of-return. When you invest your life in Jesus Christ, the benefits are infinite and perpetual while your "cost" is zero. However, the true "cost" was **_huge_** and was paid by God Himself when He sent His only begotten Son – Jesus Christ – to be the perfect and complete atoning sacrifice for our sins. Using our formula, we find:

$$\text{rate-of-return} = +\infty/0 = \text{an infinite rate-of-return}$$

There are other rewards available to the Christian. John 14:2 tells us that God is preparing a beautiful mansion for each Christian. Philippians 4:19 states: "And my God will meet all your needs according to his glorious riches in Christ Jesus." (NIV). This is one of the greatest promises on earth and represents a **_blank check_** for our basic necessities. Furthermore, heaven is above and beyond our most expansive imagination. Both the Old and New Testaments declare that the human eye has not seen, nor the ear heard; in fact, it has not even entered into the heart of man, the things that God has prepared for those who love Him. (Isaiah 64:4 and I Corinthians 2:9).

From an investment perspective, no investment provides a better rate of return than accepting Christ as one's Messiah. In fact, no other investment has any eternal benefits. God is on your side and does not desire that any person should perish but that everyone should come to repentance. (II Peter 3:9).

Salvation is a free gift. In Romans 6:23 (KJV), Paul stated: *"For the wages of sin is death but the **gift** of God is eternal life through Jesus Christ our Lord."* While the gift is free, it must be **_accepted_** by each individual. An adage throughout the investment community is: "If it seems too good to be true, it probably is."

However, in this case, what seems too good to be true is, in fact, **_absolutely true_**. Jesus himself said: *"Come unto me, all ye that labour* *and are heavy laden, and I will give you rest. Take my yoke upon you, and learn of me; for I am meek and lowly in heart; and ye shall find rest unto your souls. For my yoke is easy, and my burden is light."* Matthew 11:28-30 (KJV). Also, in His "Pastoral Discourse," Jesus declared: *"Peace I leave with you, my peace I give unto you: not as the world giveth, give I unto you. Let not your heart be troubled, neither let it be afraid."* John 14:27, (KJV).

In following God's commands, Paul said in Romans 12:1: *"Therefore, I urge you, brothers, in view of God's mercy, to offer your bodies as living sacrifices, holy and pleasing to God—this is your spiritual* [reasonable (KJV)] *act of worship."* (NIV). The word which is translated "reasonable" in that passage is the Greek word— *"lŏgikŏs."* It is the root word for logical. Therefore, it is only logical and rational to accept Jesus as one's Lord and Savior.

An ungodly heresy is that all religions lead to God just as many roads lead to Dallas. However, that argument does not hold up when it is compared to what Christ said. *"Jesus answered, 'I am **the** way and **the** truth and **the** life. No one comes to the Father except through me.'"* [John 14:6, NIV] {emphasis added}. That position is further amplified in Acts 4:12 which states: *"Salvation is found in no one else, for there is no other name under heaven given to men by which we must be saved."* [NIV] Obviously, in light of God's Word, the one and only road to God is through Christ who was also God.

Therefore, if your life is not in harmony with God's desire, you should accept Jesus as your Messiah. To receive Christ as your personal savior, pray the following prayer; then sign and date it at the bottom. When you do, you have made the absolute best investment available in the universe and the only investment which counts for eternity.

<u>*My Decision to Receive Christ As My Savior*</u>

Confessing to God that I am a sinner, and believing that the Lord Jesus Christ died for my sins on the cross and was raised for my justification, I do now receive and confess Him as my personal Savior.

Name	*Date*

3

CHAPTER 2

CHRISTIAN FINANCIAL OBJECTIVES—
THE CURE FOR FINANCIAL DEPRESSION

*"Beloved, I wish above all things that thou mayest prosper
and be in health even as thy soul prospereth."* **III John 2 (KJV)**

*"We're the best of friends, and I pray for good fortune in everything you do,
and for your good health—that your everyday affairs prosper,
as well as your soul!* **III John 2 (TM)**

What is "Financial Depression"? It is a condition where one or more of the following symptoms are present in your life:
1. You have more debt than assets.
2. There is more month than there is money.
3. Your creditors are hounding you incessantly for payments.
4. Your retirement savings have gone down to such a point that you believe that you will have to work for the rest of your life after you have already worked very hard and saved for many years.
5. You have a general "dread" about your financial future.
6. Your investments have fallen so much that you do not want to open your statement or go to the investment website to know where you actually are financially.
7. You are wondering if bankruptcy is really as bad as your preconceived notions.
8. You are continually "broke."
9. Your tax situation causes you to wake up in the middle of the night or creates other insomnia challenges.

If any of these conditions are present in your life, you may be suffering from mild or severe "Financial Depression." Praise God, there is hope! This book will present solutions for all of the above conditions. However, the solution will require: *(1) commitment, (2) hard work, and (3) follow-through* to achieve your financial goals and desires. It may not be easy for you and you may feel that the "cure" is worse than the "disease" before you reach your objectives. *Do not lose heart, it can be done when you get back to the basic principles that the Bible has for financial stability and prosperity.*

Elijah

The Word of God covers mental and emotional depression in some of its characters. The prophet Elijah is a perfect example. Elijah had experienced tremendous spiritual success in I Kings 18:16-46. After overseeing the slaughter of 450 prophets of Baal and proving that the Lord is God, Elijah experienced depression when he was informed that Jezebel was plotting to kill him. (I Kings 19:1-2) In I Kings 19:3-5 (ESV), we find the following information:

> Then he was afraid, and he arose and ran for his life and came to Beersheba which belongs to Judah, and left his servant there. But he himself went a day's journey into the wilderness and came and sat down under a broom tree. And he asked that he might die, saying, "It is enough: now O Lord, take away my life for I am no better than my fathers." And he lay down and slept under a broom tree. And behold an angel touched him and said to him, "Arise and eat."

How could Elijah have such dark thoughts that he wanted his life taken almost immediately after he had experienced such a spiritual high? The answer is that he was feeling some mental depression.

David

King David was a man after God's own heart. (Acts 13:22) However, he experienced some mental, physical, and spiritual highs and lows that most Christians cannot even imagine. In the power of the Almighty, David, while still a boy, killed Goliath single-handedly when the entire army of Israel was cowering down.

Later, King Saul pursued David to kill him as if he were a wild animal. However, the Lord protected David through the entire ordeal.

David created some unnecessary severe discomfort for himself when he became involved with Bathsheba and plotted the death of her husband, Uriah. Also, Absalom, one of David's favorite sons, planned the overthrow of his father's kingdom and almost succeeded in his scheme.

While David became a fierce, skilled, and experienced warrior in his younger years, he could not keep warm at night in his old age and had to rely on a young maiden for warmth at night. Depression was not too far from David many times during his life.

In one particularly discouraging segment of David's life when he was fleeing Absalom's rebellion, the following verse in II Samuel 15:30 (NIV) paints a vivid picture of King David's bitter mental depression.

But David continued up the Mount of Olives, weeping as he went; his head was covered and he was barefoot. All of the people with him covered their heads too and were weeping as they went up.

Please visualize King David weeping (not crying), no foot coverings, probably sweaty, dirty, smelly, and perhaps bloody from briars and other sharp objects. What a picture of degradation, heart ache, and depression.

Financial Depression

If you are experiencing financial depression, your financial depression is probably not as severe as the mental depression suffered by the prophet Elijah or King David. But, if you are suffering from financial depression, it is very real to you. If you would like to do something about it, please keep reading. There are some cures and benefits ahead for every person. God is so good. He is so good to me and wants to help you as well.

Starting the Cure and Benefits

An old adage is: "to fail to plan is to plan to fail." Many people are proving the truth of that maxim with their failure to plan financially.

Bankruptcies are close to historic highs. Unfortunately, some of those financial failures are Christians. Many Christians' failures have come as a direct result of their poor financial plans or their total lack of planning. Other Christians have "financial plans" but, either through ignorance or lack of carry-through, those individuals do not reach their highest financial potential. However, with the extremely high cost of basic commodities and the economic malaise being felt throughout the world, some financial failures are completely beyond the control of the individual.

Actually, financial difficulties may hinder a Believer's spiritual maturity, discipleship, and Christian witness. Almost all Christians could improve their personal financial management. The purpose of this book is to present Biblical principles of finance and examples of how to apply those principles so that all Christians can mature in the Lord Jesus Christ and serve HIM at their highest capability.

Priorities

In all activities, priorities should be established so that the most important task may be accomplished first. Then, the next most important task may be done. After that, all succeeding activities should be completed in sequence according to their relative importance.

In the "Sermon on the Mount," Jesus established Christian priorities when he stated, *"Seek ye first the Kingdom of God, and His righteousness; and all these things shall be added unto you."* (Matthew 6:33, KJV). That admonition applies to all areas of the Christian's life and has an especially important application in financial affairs. We must put Christ first in our financial plans just as we do in all other activities. Therefore, we must pray for God's guiding hand in our financial plans for the greatest spiritual blessing.

The essence of Christian financial planning priorities can be found in James 4:13-16 [NIV]:

> *"Now listen you who say, 'Today or tomorrow we will go to this or that city, spend a year there, carry on business and make money.' Why, you do not even know what will happen tomorrow. What is your life? You are a mist that appears for a little while and then vanishes. Instead, you ought to say, '**If it is the Lord's will**, we will live and do this or that.' As it is, you boast and brag. All such boasting is evil."* [Emphasis added.]

8

We must always seek God's will for our financial dealings to be blessed by the Lord. Prayer and seeking God's will are the highest priority items for any proposed financial consideration. Acting outside of God's divine plan will generally lead to heartache, pain, and financial disappointment ultimately.

Personal Commitment

Mastery of one's financial affairs requires personal commitment or desire just as it does in other endeavors. In the fifth chapter of the gospel according to John, Jesus met a man at the healing pool of Bethesda who had been crippled for 38 years. Apparently, throughout the years, there was no one to place him into the water at the right time for whatever medical benefits that the water might provide. In the context of John 5, it seems obvious that the man was interested in being healed. However, ***Jesus did not*** assume that and asked the man, *"Do you wish to get well?"* (John 5:6b, NASB). Jesus wanted the man to proclaim his desire and commitment for healing.

Some people are seemingly proud of their medical maladies or financial difficulties. God expects seekers to do more than simply "talk" about healing or resolving their financial affairs. He expects personal commitment and action to "cure" the situation.

In the area of finances, each Christian must answer the following question: ***"Do you REALLY want to get your financial affairs in order?"*** (How sincere is your personal commitment to resolve the challenge?) Until that question is answered affirmatively with a solid commitment, no real progress can be made to work out one's finances. Therefore, each Christian must genuinely desire to get his/her financial house in order before that undertaking will be beneficial. An earnest commitment may require some difficult and unpleasant decisions to be made and implemented. The person who truly wants financial stability must be prepared to accept some pain in the realization of a financial game plan. Temporarily, the "cure may seem worse than the disease." However, with commitment, time, and effort, financial equilibrium can be achieved.

Christian Financial Objectives

What is the proper financial goal for a Christian? Should you aim to be very rich or poor as a "church mouse?" Is wealth inherently evil? What are the caveats or warnings that are in order concerning the Christian and wealth? These questions and others will be addressed in this section.

First of all, there are two fallacies or heresies which are sometimes found in Christian circles. One fallacy states that no wealthy person can achieve spiritual maturity. It is sometimes exaggerated to state that a wealthy person cannot be a Christian. On the other hand, there is a segment of Christianity which believes that a poverty-stricken Christian is a spiritual giant because of his/her economic condition. As we progress, it will be clear that both positions, per se, are incorrect. Although, there are wealthy people who have little or no regard for the things of God while there are relatively poor people who desire to live in the center of God's will.

Economic position does not determine a person's spirituality.

John's Desire for Gaius

In the final analysis, it is very difficult to improve on John's wish or prayer for Gaius when he said, *"Beloved, I wish above all things that thou mayest prosper and be in health even as thy soul prospereth."* (III John 2, KJV). There is perhaps nothing better on earth for a Christian than to enjoy good health and prosperity of the soul as God blesses that person financially. III John 2 is the verse that I pray for each reader.

The Sayings of Agur, Son of Jakeh

In the 30th chapter of Proverbs (KJV), Agur made a request to God that is a good goal statement for most Christians. In verse 8, he requested, *"...give me neither poverty nor riches..."* His reasoning is explained in verse 9 where he stated, *"Lest I be full, and deny thee, and say, Who is the Lord? Or lest I be poor, and steal, and take the name of God in vain."*

From those two verses, we can see that the two economic extremes are hazardous for Christians. Only the strongest of Christians can function well at either extreme. Being in the "middle class" is comfortable for most and in line with Scripture. Let us, therefore, consider the concepts of poverty and wealth from a Biblical perspective.

Biblical Examples of Poverty

Jesus

Jesus experienced great agony on the cross for our sins and also suffered in many other ways. He willingly left all of the unimaginable wealth of heaven for economic sparseness on earth. In Matthew 8:20 [NIV], Jesus said, *"Foxes have holes and birds of the air have nests, but the Son of Man has no place to lay his head."* Jesus typically relied on others for shelter and had little more than the clothes on his back. Jesus probably would have been counted in the "homeless" census and would have undoubtedly qualified with those below the "poverty line" of today.

Lazarus

In the 16th chapter of Luke, Jesus relates the story of a man named Lazarus and a rich man. This Lazarus is not the same one that Jesus raised from the dead but was a beggar who was covered with sores which the dogs licked. Lazarus was so poor that he longed to eat the crumbs which fell from the rich man's dining table. Some scholars consider this story to be a parable. However, if so, it is the only parable where Jesus gave a name to one of the characters In time, the rich man died and was delivered to a location where he was *"in agony in this fire"* (hell). Also, Lazarus passed away and *"the angels carried him to Abraham's side"* (heaven). After that, in Luke 16:25, the narrative addresses the rich man's request for cooling water by stating, *"But Abraham replied, 'Son, remember that in your* [the rich man's] *lifetime you received your good things, while Lazarus received bad things."*

This sequence of events demonstrates dramatically that economic fortunes may be totally reversed in heaven when compared to earth. It also shows that poverty-stricken Christians may look forward to an eternity of prosperity.

God's Blessings for the Poor

In the second chapter of James, the half-brother of Jesus compared church favoritism of the rich and the poor. James chastised any church that shows unfair preferential treatment toward the wealthy. In James 2:5-7 (NIV), he stated:

Listen, my dear brothers: Has not God chosen those who are poor in the eyes of the world to be rich in faith and to inherit the kingdom he promised those who love him? But you have insulted the poor. Is it not the rich who are exploiting you? Are they not the ones who are dragging you into court? Are they not the ones who are slandering the noble name of him to whom you belong?

Further in the passage at James 2:9-10 (NIV), James condemns favoritism by emphasizing:

But if you show favoritism, you sin and are convicted by the law as lawbreakers. For whoever keeps the whole law and yet stumbles at just one point is guilty of breaking all of it.

Clearly, James has strong denunciation against favoritism for the rich and discrimination aimed at the poor.

In the Old Testament, David demonstrated God's concern for the poor in Psalm 12:5 (REB): *'Now I will arise,' says the Lord, 'for the poor are being plundered, the needy groan; I shall place them in the safety for which they long.'* The Mosaic law had many specific provisions for the benefit of the poor.[1] In fact, God promised Israel that there would be *"no poor among you,"* if they obeyed the voice of the Lord.[2] The conclusions concerning the poor are obvious. First, both the Old and the New Testament proclaim God's provision, care, and concern for the poor. Second, in God's economy, there is absolutely no stigma attached to being poor as long as that person is obeying the Word of God. Therefore, Christians with low economic status should be treated as first-class citizens of the bride of Christ (the church) and receive no discriminatory treatment.

Solomon's Economic Position

Solomon was greatly blessed by God and was the wealthiest man of his day. In fact, there is evidence to show that he was the wealthiest of any day. (II Chronicles 1:12). However, in Ecclesiastes, his heart cry that all is vanity and vexation *"under the sun"* is a somber warning to anyone contemplating riches for riches sake.

Others

In the Old Testament, Boaz was described as a mighty man of wealth.[3] Job had immense wealth but lost it all in a time of great testing from Satan. However, after the time of testing was over, God restored Job's blessings more in the latter part of Job's life than the first.[4] In the New Testament, Joseph of Arimathea was described by Matthew as being a rich man.[5] For *both* power and wealth, Daniel ruled over the whole province of Babylon and was chief of the governors over all of the wise men of Babylon.[6]

Conclusions on Economic Position

Economic position is totally irrelevant as far as God's spiritual blessings are concerned. Many wealthy men have contributed directly or indirectly to the furtherance of God's Kingdom throughout the centuries. Both the Old and New Testaments have examples.

On the other hand, God loves and cares for the poor. The Bible declares that: *"Indeed there are those who are last who will be first, and first who will be last."*[7] However, there is assurance that all Christians will have their needs met by God. Also, there is a propensity toward prosperity as we shall see in the next section.

Christian Propensity Toward Prosperity

The greatest promise of security for the Christian is found in Paul's letter to the Philippian Church. There, Paul, firmly proclaims, *"But my God shall supply all of your need according to his riches in glory by Christ Jesus."* (Philippians 4:19, KJV). King David expressed the same idea in the Old Testament in Psalm 23:1 (KJV) when he said, *"The Lord is my shepherd; I shall not want."* God is going to meet our needs on this earth or call us home to our glorious reward. After our time is completed on earth, God will present us with our beautiful mansion in heaven where there is no more sickness, pain, or tears.   God will either meet our needs on earth or honor us with heaven. It is a "win-win" situation for the Christian. Moreover, there are some built-in economic advantages for the Christian.

In Colossians 3:23 [NIV], we are admonished: *"Whatever you do, work at it with all your heart, as working for the Lord, not for men."* In other words, do everything as if you were doing it for the Lord and not for men. Because of the laws of physics, "cream rises to the top." Although this is a physical law, it also has application in the economic arena. Joseph is a prime example of "cream rising to the top." Even though Joseph was sold into slavery by his brothers, he eventually was purchased by Potiphar, the captain of the guard of the Pharaoh of Egypt which was the foremost country in the world at that time. In the 39th chapter of Genesis, Potiphar saw the kind of work Joseph did and also that God was with Joseph. Joseph was then promoted over all of the attendants of Potiphar to be entrusted with everything that Potiphar owned. In effect, Joseph was second in command for Potiphar's estate immediately below Potiphar himself.

In a lengthy story that spans thirteen chapters in Genesis, Joseph was **_falsely accused_** by Potiphar's wife and put in prison. While in prison, he was betrayed by his prison friend and had additional undeserved difficulties. Once again, "cream rose to the top" and Joseph was eventually promoted from "prisoner to Prime Minister" in an instant by the Pharaoh. Joseph did everything with his "heart" and, as a result, enjoyed immense economic success in the end.

Will all Christians enjoy the same type of success that Joseph experienced? The answer may not always be "yes." However, by working with all of our "heart," there is no limit to how far we can go up the economic ladder.

This same thought is further amplified in Proverbs. There, Solomon declares, *"Lazy hands make a man poor, but diligent hands bring wealth."* (Proverbs 10:4, NIV). When a Christian puts "heart" into his/her work, there is a tendency to prosper. Furthermore, in his description of the God-fearing man, David declared that

"whatsoever he doeth shall prosper." [8]

Because there are so many passages that deal with prosperity, many mistakenly believe that once a person becomes a Christian that person will automatically become "healthy, wealthy, and wise." All problems will vanish and everything will become a bed of roses. In many instances, the exact opposite occurs because Satan will come out to challenge the "defector" from his camp. In the first two chapters of Job, God allowed Satan to take everything that Job had except his wife and she proved to be less than helpful.

Clearly, there is abundant evidence to support the position that there is a tendency for the Christian to become prosperous. There is, however, no guarantee that this will occur and faithful Christians may enjoy less than complete prosperity and still be in the center of God's will. This is borne out in the story of Lazarus and the rich man which was covered earlier in this chapter.

Conditional Promises

In addition to the absolute promises already covered, there are some conditional promises of prosperity. These promises are conditioned on the Christian fulfilling some specific requirement. One of the most powerful conditional promises ever given is found when God spoke to Joshua about leading the children of Israel into Canaan after Moses's death.

In Joshua 1:8 [NIV], the Lord commanded the mighty general by saying, *"Do not let this Book of the Law depart out of your mouth; meditate on it day and night, so that you may be careful to do everything written in it. Then you will be prosperous and successful."* (Emphasis added.) **WHAT A PROMISE!** The secret to the two characteristics: prosperity and success, which rational people seek, are contained in that passage. However, both prosperity and success are conditioned on meditation and application of God's Word. But, those achievements are not automatic and are conditional.

Similar passages are found in the Bible but the grandeur of Joshua 1:8 is lofty and inspiring. Another passage contains the promise concerning the covenant that God made with the children of Israel in the land of Moab when He stated, *"Carefully follow the terms of this covenant, so that you may prosper in everything you do."* [9] When King David turned his throne over to Solomon, he charged him saying,

"So be strong, show yourself a man, and observe what the Lord your God requires: Walk in his ways, and keep his decrees and commands, his laws and requirements, as written in the Law of Moses, so that you may prosper in all you do and wherever you go." (I Kings 2b-3, NIV).

After reviewing the passages in the Bible concerning prosperity and success, what are conclusions which can be drawn? First, we must "walk in His ways." As Mary, the mother of Jesus, told the servants at the wedding feast of Cana: **"Do** *whatever he tells you."* [Emphasis added.] (John 2:5, NIV). Therefore, obedience is the first ingredient in obtaining prosperity and success.

Second, we must keep his "decrees, commands, laws, and requirements." We must be in the "center of His will" and obey His leading. As the prophet Samuel told King Saul in I Samuel 15:22b [NIV], *"To obey is better than sacrifice, and to heed is better than the fat of rams."* "Walking in His ways" and obeying His will are mandatory for prosperity and success.

Caveats Concerning Wealth

While there are many Scripture passages that promote wealth, there are some which warn against the misuse of wealth. Perhaps the most familiar and misquoted caveat is found in I Timothy 6:10 (NIV). Some say: "Money is the root of all evil." Actually, money is a neutral commodity. Money builds churches; sends missionaries to foreign and domestic fields; pays for evangelistic programs and other Christian activities. The correct citation is: *"For the love of money is the root of all evil..."* When a person elevates money to the position of an idol and, it takes preeminence over God, then it becomes very wicked. In effect, that belief breaks the first commandment of the Ten Commandments which is: *"Thou shalt have no other gods before me."* (KJV). When money becomes a god, it is always a sin.

Another solemn warning comes from the lips of Jesus when he stated that: *"It is easier for a camel to go through the eye of a needle, than for a rich man to enter into the Kingdom of God."* [10] This is a very important declaration because it is included in 3 of the 4 gospels. Also, there are various interpretations of that statement. One popular idea is that it is totally absurd for a man bound up in his riches to expect to enter the Kingdom of God. As the camel was the largest animal found in Palestine and the eye of a needle one of the smallest openings, it would be impossible for this to occur. It may have been simple hyperbole.

Another interpretation was that the "eye of a needle" was the relatively small opening in a city wall and a camel might have to go to his knees (assume a humble state) or offload some of its goods (reduce the amount of wealth) to enter. In the context of The Message, Eugene Peterson seems to believe that the Holy Spirit must achieve the goal for us. Regardless of the interpretation, reasonable people would agree that there is stern counsel and caution concerning proper wealth stewardship. Perhaps it means something different for each of us and God's Holy Spirit must provide the interpretation for each of us individually.

In another vein, the human writer of Psalm 49 presents wealth in a different light and states:

> *Why should I fear when evil days come, when wicked deceivers surround me—those who trust in their wealth and boast of their great riches? No man can redeem the life of another or give to God a ransom for him—the ransom for a life is costly, no payment is ever enough—that he should live on forever and not see decay. For all can see that wise men die; the foolish and the senseless alike perish and leave their wealth to others."* (Psalm 49:5-10, NIV)

Only the blood of Jesus Christ can provide salvation. Wealth will always be taken from us. We can elect to use it on this earth to promote the Kingdom of Heaven or others will use it for their purposes after we pass on. The choice is ours.

For "self-made" men who believe, "my power and the might of mine hand hath gotten me this wealth," Moses reminds them of a very important point. *"But remember the Lord your God, for it is he who gives you the ability to produce wealth."* [11]

Actually, everything belongs to God. He simply lets us use His resources during our brief time on earth. Under the influence of God's Holy Spirit, Asaph spoke for God saying, *"...for every animal of the forest is mine and the cattle on a thousand hills...If I were hungry I would not tell you for the world is mine, and all that is in it."* (Psalm 50:10 & 12, NIV).

At the same time, God does not give prosperity to some because *"...the prosperity of fools shall destroy them."* Conversely, those who *"hearkeneth unto me shall dwell safely, and shall be quiet from fear of evil."* (Proverbs 1:32-33, KJV)

Chapter Summary

In any endeavor, **_priorities_** are critical. When we put God first in accordance with Matthew 6:33 and the first commandment of the Ten Commandments, our financial affairs will begin to take shape. In addition, each person must have a very strong personal **_commitment_** to work diligently on his/her finances in accordance with God's will and the assistance of God's Holy Spirit. Christian financial adjustments may be painful.

While there is a bias toward prosperity in the Bible, many of God's most precious promises are directed to the poor. If a Christian does obtain wealth, there are many Biblical **_warnings_** which must be carefully considered. Many of God's prosperity promises are **_conditional_** on our actions or obedience.

CHAPTER 3

FINANCIAL PLANNING—
A FINANCIAL GAME PLAN THAT BRINGS
HONOR & GLORY TO GOD

"For which one of you, when he wants to build a tower,
does not first sit down and calculate the cost, to see if he has
enough to complete it?" **Luke 14:28 (NASB)**

"Or what king, going to make war against another king, does not sit down
first and consider whether he is able with ten thousand to meet him who comes
against him with twenty thousand?" **Luke 14:31 (NKJV)**

"Let all things be done decently and in order" **I Corinthians 14:40 (KJV)**

Once specific financial objectives have been determined, then action must be taken to reach those objectives. Effective ***follow-through*** will determine whether there is a genuine desire to achieve the financial target or simply a superficial wish "to talk" about goals. Before looking at specific methods of plan applications, let us look at passages dealing with prayer and planning from the Bible.

Jesus & Prayer

Before any endeavor or choice, prayer should precede it. We are told in I Thessalonians 5:17 (KJV) to: *"Pray without ceasing."* Jesus prayed in every situation. In the garden of Gethsemane, Jesus prayed:

*And he went a little farther, and fell on his face, and **prayed**,*
saying O my Father, if it be possible, let this cup pass from me:
nevertheless not as I will, but as thou wilt. Matthew 26:39
(KJV), [Emphasis added.]

Jesus prayed that the "cup" [His agony and suffering on the cross]
might be removed from Him in favor of some other alternative.
However, He also prayed that the Father's will be done. Ultimately,
Jesus became the perfect sacrifice and went to the cross to pay the sin
debt that each of us owes. But, Jesus prayed continually before going
to the cross.

Jesus provided the example of prayer for all of us. He prayed before
meals and every event. There is a lesson for each of us here. We need
to pray before anything else is done. Too many Christians (this writer
previously included) make decisions and **then** ask God to bless those
decisions. We need to "pray it through" and seek God's divine will
before any endeavor. This is critically important in any financial plan
or decision.

Jesus & Planning

In the 14th Chapter of Luke, Jesus spoke concerning the requirements
of discipleship. During that discourse, he spoke of two situations
requiring planning. Both illustrations have direct application to financial
plans. From each, we can determine that Christ included planning in
every activity and He considered it a necessary requirement for any
contemplated venture.

In the first example, Jesus said:

For which one of you, when he wants to build a tower, does not
*first sit down and **calculate** the cost, to see if he has enough to*
complete it? Otherwise, when he had laid a foundation, and is
not able to finish, all who observe it begin to ridicule him, saying,
'This man began to build and was not able to finish.'[1]

This example dealt with a capital expenditure for a tower. However,
it could have been a financial plan for July instead of a capital expenditure
for a tower. Planning is appropriate and, generally necessary, for any
financial decision.

Jesus further amplified and drove the point of planning home in the second parable. There, Christ admonished:

> *Or what king, when he sets out to meet another king in battle, will not first sit down and take counsel whether he is strong enough with ten thousand men to counter the one coming against him with twenty thousand? Or else, while the other is still far away, sends a delegation and asks terms of peace.*[2]

Anything that is repeated twice in God's Word is important. Therefore, because of the two back-to-back parables that Jesus proclaimed—one dealing with a "planned capital expenditure" for a tower and the other dealing with a "battle plan"—it seems reasonable and logical for every Christian to have a financial plan.

Planning for Investment

In his discussion of a "wife of noble character," Solomon emphasized the business potential for wives. During that discourse, Solomon proclaimed: *"She considers a field and buys it; out of her earnings she plants a vineyard."*[3] The word for "considers" is the Hebrew word—*zamam*—which means "to plan." In the context of the sentence, it implies that she is comparing that field to other available fields and that field to alternative investments. In short, she is carefully contemplating her investment and consummating the purchase after she is satisfied that the proposed investment is sound. This is another example of how relevant planning is for financial improvement.

Financial Vision

In Proverbs, Solomon declared, *"Where there is no vision [no redemptive revelation of God], the people perish."*[4] According to Strong's Concordance, the word for vision comes from the Hebrew word: *"chazown"* which means mental image, dream, revelation, or oracle.[5] A Christian who lacks financial stability needs to visualize, mentally, a stable, healthy financial position and aim for that goal. While it would be very rare for a person to "perish" because of the lack of a financial game plan, a Christian's life should be "more abundant" and lacking some of the frustrations that are prevalent with economic chaos. After "praying it through," Christians need to develop a sound financial vision for the future.

Planning Priorities

In planning, as in any activity involving two or more endeavors, priorities should be determined for maximum efficiency. Solomon, the man with the greatest wisdom on earth, said: *"Prepare your work outside, get everything ready for you in the field; and after that build your house."* [6] In the Living Bible, the editors paraphrased that verse to make it clear by stating, *"Develop your business first before building your house."* [7] This proverb shows that the fruits produced by business endeavors provide the means for personal goals such as building a house. The converse is not true. Building a house, however, will not bring capital into a business undertaking.

The Lord's Role in Planning

Earlier in this chapter, we looked at the role of prayer in financial planning. When we pray, we must be willing for God to overrule our plans and say "no" when our prayer request is not best for us. His sovereign will is always going to provide the best spiritual benefits even if it does not appear that way at first. Solomon declared that when he said: *"In his heart a man plans his course, but the Lord determines his steps."* [8] The Revised English Bible renders that verse to state: *"Someone may plan his journey by his own wit, but it is the Lord who guides his steps."* [9]

This position is reinforced by James in his general epistle. Eugene Peterson uses up-to-date vernacular when he states:

> *And now I have a word for you who brashly announce, "Today—at the latest tomorrow—we're off to such and such a city for the year. We're going to start a business and make a lot of money." You don't know the first thing about tomorrow. You're nothing but a wisp of fog, catching a brief bit of sun before disappearing. Instead, make it a habit to say, "**If the Master wills it** and we're still alive, we'll do this or that."* [10] [Emphasis added.]

We must always consider the Lord's Will before we do anything.

Determining Current Position

To determine future goals, it is necessary for us to determine our current position. After the current position has been calculated, then a tailor-made individual (or family unit) "financial game plan" (FGP) can be developed. It is a relatively easy to determine a person's net personal equity or "net worth."

First, for a specific date—December 31, 2009 or July 31, 2010, as an example—list all assets (economic resources) or asset categories and the approximate current value for each asset or category. Microsoft Excel or other spread sheet programs work very well for this task. Categories for items such as clothing might be grouped into a "clothing" account rather than listing each individual item. Clothing may be listed as a minimum amount because clothing is generally considered to be a "sunk cost." A sunk cost is one that cannot typically be recovered once the expenditure is made. However, major items, such as motor vehicles should be listed separately with a conservative valuation.

Any projected future "cash-flows" (such as Social Security, Railroad Retirement, etc.) should be detailed in narrative form separately without being added to the asset list. Those items should have the starting date, monthly amount, and any other relevant information for each item.

Second, list all of the principal amounts of debts (liabilities or obligations owed) along with annual percentage interest rate (APR), required monthly payment (or other payment schedule) and any other specific requirements such as a future "balloon payment." If there is any accrued interest owed, that interest should be listed as a separate item and labeled appropriately. Any contingent liabilities (such as co-signing on a note payable) should be described separately in detailed narrative form without being added to the debt list.

Last, the total amount of debts should be subtracted from the total amount of assets. The resulting figure is net personal equity or "net worth." There may be two types of surprises that result from this exercise. First, some people discover, with pleasure, that they are much wealthier than they had realized previously. That is exciting good news for those people. However, some realize, to their chagrin that their financial condition is very precarious and a great deal of work needs to be done. In some cases, ***immediate effort*** is required. A third group will be pleased to note that they are making good progress along life's financial pathway and that very little or no adjustment is necessary.

An example of the net personal equity calculation is shown below:

"Richard Redeemed" (or Richard Redeemed Family Unit)
Personal (or Family) Balance Sheet
December 31, 2009

Assets (listed separately at current value)	$ XX	
[as of Dec. 31, 2009]	XX	
	$Total	$200,000
- Debts Owed (listed separately)	$ XX	
[as of Dec. 31, 2009]	XX	
	$Total	- $ 50,000
= Difference (net personal equity)		=$150,000

The net personal equity position represents the equity that a person (or family unit) has in his/her (their) assets. Once the net personal equity figure has been calculated, it serves as a standard by which financial progress can be measured.

Once net personal equity has been determined, then, that net personal equity can be compared with another point in time to evaluate the progress that has been made. For example, if total assets equal $100,000 at December 31, 2009 and debts total $50,000, then net personal equity is $50,000. One year later, if assets total $110,000 and debts total $45,000, then the net equity position is $65,000 and has increased $15,000 from the previous point in time. In that manner, financial progress can be determined.

Also, another valuable analysis is to compare the last 3 years tax returns on a computer spread sheet such as Microsoft Excel. This calculation will show the changes that have occurred to revenue streams and deductions. This exercise may also suggest modifications or changes that need to be made.

Financial Game Plan or (FGP)

A Balance Sheet Approach

To assist you in reaching your financial goal, you should prepare an FGP. An FGP is a system whereby a person's net personal equity is planned in advance. With our formula:

Assets – Debts = Net Personal Equity,

There are basically two ways that we can increase net personal equity. First, we can increase assets while holding debt constant. A perfect example occurs when the value of a residence goes up while the mortgage does not change significantly. Second, we can decrease debt and hold assets constant. This occurs when debt is paid down and no additional debts are incurred. Another possibility occurs when there is some variation of the first and second cases simultaneously.

A Cash-Flow Approach

Viewing net personal equity from an inflow-outgo concept, there are only two ways that net personal equity can be increased—revenues must be increased or expenditures must be decreased. Stated another way, you must "earn more or spend less." Again, it is normal for there to be some combination of the two which will increase net personal equity.

There are numerous FGP's. Some are quite simple while others are exceedingly complex. The proper one for you is the one that is comfortable in application and achieves your goal.

All FGP's have at least one common element—comparison. Basically, you will be comparing what _you planned to do_ with what _you actually did_. The following illustration shows a model for FGP application:

"Richard Redeemed"
FGP
for the month of July, 2009

Item	Planned	Actual	Difference	Explanation
Salary-after deductions	$2500	$2600	+$100	Bonus
All other revenues & inflows listed	$ 600	$ 100	- $500	Rental Unit Vacant
Total	$3100	$2700	- $400	
All expenditures Listed	$ XX	$ XX	$ XX	Unexpected Auto Repair
Total	$2400	$2600	+$200	
Net	$ 700	$ 100	- $600	

Regulation or Limitation

The primary purpose of an FGP is ***control over financial planning***. If that goal is not achieved through an FGP, then the *formal* FGP should be revised to achieve the necessary financial control. Some people live long, happy, and prosperous lives without a formal FGP. They have internalized their FGP and control cash flows intrinsically. If that method works well for you, then "go for it." However, if you are one of the thousands who must live from "hand-to-mouth" and continually have "more month than they have cash" in their accounts, then some type of formal FGP may be the answer to prayer for you.

FGP Mechanics

Some people control their expenditures by placing specific amounts of money in various envelopes. They place $500 in an envelope marked "rent;" $350 in an envelope marked "food;" and so forth until all of the cash has been distributed. They can spend up to the amount in each envelope until it is gone. Then, the envelope marked "save" is deposited in some financial institution or invested. The "envelope approach" provides control over expenditures.

However, there are some serious flaws in the "envelope approach." First, the money in the envelopes could be stolen. In this day and age, it is still a good policy never to carry more cash than you can afford to lose. That is a good policy for money kept around the house also. Second, "over-expenditure" requires a system of inter-envelope transfers or bank loans and tends to make the system somewhat unwieldy. But, the *concept* of the envelope system transfers over into a better approach.

A better approach is to record all revenues and expenses into a good computer spreadsheet such as Microsoft Excel and control in that way. Every situation is unique and should be tailored to each specific situation.

How much should be planned for each expenditure? While there are few "concrete" guidelines, except for the tithe, [This will be covered in more detail later.], Table 3-1 may provide some helpful insights for an FGP. Actually, some of the benefits that can be derived from this exercise may be to force you to make some choices based on your individual situation. For example, if you desire a nicer, more expensive home, then your diet and recreation choices may have to be re-evaluated. If your clothing choices run on the expensive side, then some other choice(s) may need reduction. However, all expenditures and savings must equal 100% of available cash or progress cannot be made.

Also, historically high prices for energy and commodities are adversely affecting plans for many people. However, with each new challenge, modifications must be incorporated into existing plans.

Table 3-1
Expenditure Guidelines

	Percent
Tithes and Offerings	10-15
Housing	25-30
Food	20-25
Clothing	5-10
Medical Care	3-6
Recreation	2-4
Personal Care	1-2
Miscellaneous	4-6
Savings and Investments	10-20
Available Cash	100

The expenditure guidelines in Table 3-1 require some explanations. First the principal variable is the amount going to savings. Savings should have a common element with tithes and offerings for individuals or families starting out—both should not go below 10 percent. However, both may be greater. Obviously, all people will not allocate their funds in the same way and the guidelines are intended to be flexible rather than rigid. The proof of a successful FGP is the increase in net personal equity from year to year. Ultimately, you will discover what the "norm" is for you and your family.

By comparing actual expenditures with projected outlays, you can isolate where financial "leaks" are occurring and take appropriate action to remedy the situation. Also, the sum of all of the monthly savings and investments should help to account for the increase in net personal equity. (This increase [or decrease] will include the appreciation [or decline in value] of assets or favorable settlement of debts.

Chapter Summary

Prayer is essential for Christian financial success. Planning, formal or informal, is also a required ingredient. As a result of planning, you may initiate a "financial game plan" or FGP. The purpose of the FGP is to regulate expenditures and plan the systematic change of net personal equity. Once this is done, a Christian may turn his attention to spreading the gospel, producing fruit, and growing as a disciple. Generally, when a person's financial affairs are abused or neglected, other areas of a person's life are less effective than they could be. This condition can affect a marriage, interpersonal-relationships, and other aspects of life. The financial aspects of the Christian's life need to be handled in this way: *"Let all things be done decently and in order."* (I Corinthians 14:40, KJV).

CHAPTER 4

EMPLOYMENT—FINDING SATISFACTION & GOD'S WILL IN THE WORK PLACE

"The Lord God took man and put him in the Garden of Eden to <u>work</u> it and take care of it" **Genesis 2:15 (NIV)**

"You will eat of the produce of the field, and only by the <u>sweat of your brow</u> will you win your bread…" **Genesis 3:18b-19a (NEB)**

"Make it your ambition to lead a quiet life, to mind your own business and to <u>work</u> with your hands…" **I Thessalonians 4:11 (NIV)**

"For even when we were with you, we gave you this rule: "If a man <u>will not work</u>, he shall not eat." **II Thessalonians 3:10 (NIV)**

[Emphasis added in each case.]

Over a lifetime, most Christians will generate the lion's share of their revenue from employment. Some may work for themselves and serve others while most will be employees. Because employment is so important, and may provide the springboard for other financial opportunities, it is essential to determine what God's Word has to say about employment. In addition to the financial aspects of employment, work may provide a great sense of pleasure or be a "necessary evil." Therefore, Biblical enlightenment should provide benefits necessary to overcome some of the misconceptions surrounding the Christian and "the job."

Job Origination

Man was created, among other things, to work. In Genesis 2:15, we read: *"The Lord God put the man in the garden of Eden to care for it and work it."* (NCV). In addition, one of the by-products of Adam's original sin was man's commandment to work. The woman was given sorrow in childbirth but man was given hard work. In verse 19 of Chapter 3 of Genesis, God told Adam: *"By the sweat of your brow you will eat your food."* (NIV). On the basis of that verse, Christians are required to work. Consequently, we should make the best of it and relish our position whenever we can.

The New Testament further amplified what is covered in Genesis 3:19. In Paul's first epistle to the church at Thessalonica, he stated: *"Stay calm; mind your own business; do your own job."* [1] Also, Paul added this admonition in his second epistle to the Thessalonians: *"Already during our stay with you we laid down this rule: anyone who will not work shall not eat."* (II Thessalonians 3:10, NEB). Once again, both the Old and New Testament confirm each other by requiring honest work.

Job Determination

One of the most perplexing challenges that many young people face is that of determining what their life's work should be. Some have numerous employment positions and/or careers during a lifetime. In the end analysis, *"The steps of a man are established by the Lord; And He delights in his way."* [2] However, there is considerable effort necessary to prepare for the "right place" that God has for many Christians. All honorable jobs are necessary. In Ephesians 4:11-12, Paul declared: *"And He gave some as apostles, and some as prophets, and some as evangelists, and some as pastors and teachers, for the equipping of the saints for the work of service, to the building up of the body of Christ."* (NASB). Of course, Paul was referring to the spiritual jobs that were to be assigned. However, the same principle applies to other "tent-making" jobs. Christians should pray and attempt to match their God-given talents with the work that is needed and the position that provides true service. For an effective economy, many different jobs are necessary and Christians can be "good" or "poor" witnesses in any honorable job.

The Bible is replete with callings and jobs that God's people have had. Jesus was a carpenter; while the Apostle Paul was a tentmaker and Peter was a professional fisherman. Matthew was a tax-collector. The common employment thread throughout the Bible was endless variety. Therefore, it is only reasonable to believe that Christians have the same freedom today.

At the same time, all believers are ministers. The only question is whether you are to be a full-time minister or not. In every employment opportunity, Christians are either effective or ineffective witnesses and ministers.

Zeal for Work

Christians are admonished to: *"Do everything without grumbling or argument."*[3] Zeal is the keyword for job attitude. In God's Word, many contexts suggest that servants had a position very similar to employees of today. In Paul's epistle to the Colossians, Paul gave advice to wives, husbands, children, fathers, and servants in rapid succession. In effect, Paul told the faithful to let Christ control their family and business relationships. Specifically to servants (employees), Paul admonished:

> *Servants, do what you're told by your earthly masters. And don't just do the minimum that will get you by.* **Do your best.** *Work from the heart for your real master, for God, confident that you'll get paid in full when you come into your inheritance. Keep in mind always that the ultimate Master you're serving is Christ. The sullen servant who does shoddy work will be held responsible. Being Christian doesn't cover up bad work.*[4] [Emphasis added.]

The NKJV renders verse 3:23 this way: *"And whatever you do, do it heartily as to the Lord and not unto men."* It is abundantly clear from that passage that Christians should have zest and zeal for their jobs if they are going to please God.

A very similar message was reiterated in Paul's letter to the church at Ephesus. There Paul declared:

> *Slaves obey your earthly masters with respect and fear, and with sincerity of heart, just as you would obey Christ. Obey them not only to win their favor when their eye is on you, but like*

slaves of Christ, doing the will of God from your heart. Serve wholeheartedly, as if you were serving the Lord, not men, because you know that the Lord will reward everyone for whatever good he does, whether he is slave or free.[5]

Do All to the Glory of God

Faithful service is also emphasized in Paul's epistle to the Corinthians. There, Paul advised: *"So whether you eat or drink or **whatever you do**, do it all for the glory of God."*[6] (Emphasis added.) That advice covers one's work situation as well as all other aspects of the Christian's life.

Consistent Honest Work

In the Proverbs, Solomon declared: *"He who works his land will have abundant food, but the one who chases fantasies will have his fill of poverty."*[7] Consistent honest work leads to plenty but following whims will make a person poor. In Luke 15:11-32, the parable of the lost or prodigal son found that out the hard way. In verse 13 (NIV) it states: *"Not long after that, the youngest son got together all he had, set off for a distant country and there squandered his wealth in **wild living**."* [Emphasis added.] He became so poor that he had to slop the hogs and wanted to eat "pig cuisine." Ultimately, the father welcomed the lost son back into the fold. Hard work, rather than fantasies, provides long-term benefits.

Labor and Riches

Today, many people are pushing themselves into heart-attacks, strokes, and other self-induced illnesses.

These difficulties may be due in part to a person's mental outlook and attitude toward their job. The wise king, Solomon, declared: *"Do not weary yourself to gain riches, Cease from your consideration [or understanding] of it."*[8] Many physical and mental problems could be avoided by applying that verse of Scripture.

Laziness in the Old Testament

In the Old Testament, there are numerous warnings against laziness. Some of these warnings are: *"A lazy fellow has trouble all through life;*

a good man's path is easy!" [9] *"The one who is slack in his work is brother to one who destroys."* [10] *"The sluggard's cravings will be the death of him, because his hands refuse to work;"* [11] *"Do not love sleep or you will grow poor; stay awake and you will have food to spare."* [12] Clearly, Christians cannot be lazy. Anything less than whole-hearted commitment in employment is not in the center of God's will.

Laziness in the New Testament

Laziness is also condemned in the New Testament. In the Roman letter, the inspired writer proclaimed: *"Be kindly affectioned one to another with brotherly love; in honor preferring one another; Not slothful in business; fervent in spirit; serving the Lord;"* [13] Thus, it is evident that both the Old and New Testaments command Christians to perform faithful work and avoid slothfulness.

Results of Labor

In contrast to laziness, the fruits of labor are enjoyable results. Many Scripture verses extol the virtues of work. The wisdom book of the Bible, Proverbs, states: *"Wealth from gambling quickly disappears; wealth from hard work grows."* [14] A similar thought is also found in the contrast between the one who actually labors and the one who only talks about it. There, King Solomon succinctly proclaimed: *"Work brings profit, talk brings poverty."* [15]

Accomplishment in Labor

In labor, there are psychological benefits available to the Christian. The satisfaction that accompanies a well-done job is described in the following verse: *"The desire accomplished is sweet to the soul: but it is abomination to fools to depart from evil."* [16] Therefore, in addition to monetary compensation which accrues as a result of productive labor, there are nonmonetary advantages as well.

Time is Money

Basically, physicians, attorneys, and other professional people sell their time and expertise. As a result, it is imperative that they manage their time effectively in their employment. The Bible has much inspiration concerning time. While some people who would never think of squandering their physical assets, they may waste time which may be their most valuable asset.

Time is one of the few assets where all people are given equal amounts. No one has more than 24 hours per day or seven days per week. Consequently, time must be used wisely. In Paul's letter to the Ephesians, he emphasized that we are *"...redeeming the time..."*[17] While Paul's admonition was not specifically aimed at the work situation, it has application there also. Wise and effective use of time is the key to success in many employment situations.

Another intelligent application of time is to do the right thing at the appropriate time. In that beautiful passage dealing with time, the preacher in Ecclesiastes proclaimed:

> *To every thing there is a season and a time to every purpose under heaven: a time to be born and a time to die: A time to plant, and a time to pluck up that which is planted; a time to kill and a time to heal; a time break down and a time to build up;...A time to love and a time to hate; a time of war and a time of peace...He hath made everything beautiful in his time.*[18]

Clearly, the passage stresses the importance of proper timing and the appropriate use of time.

Managerial Probability

In the preceding passages, we have seen that the Christian must work diligently to be in accordance with God's will. Once that is done, then the Christian becomes eligible to move into positions of authority and management. Some 29 centuries ago, the wisest king, Solomon declared: *"Diligence brings people to power, but laziness to forced labour"*[19] Application of a good "Christian work ethic" will allow people to move up the ladder of success. Christians may have the inside track to promotions and advancement because of their dedication to the job.

Rest

While God's Word does not condone laziness, it commands rest. In Exodus, Moses amplified the fourth commandment of the "ten commandments" in the following way:

*Remember the Sabbath day by keeping it holy. Six days you shall labor and do all your work, but the seventh day is a Sabbath to the Lord your God. On it you shall **not do any work**, neither you, nor your son or daughter, nor you manservant or maidservant, nor your animals, nor the alien within your gates. For in six days the Lord made the heavens and the earth, the sea, and all that is in them, but he rested on the seventh day. Therefore, the Lord blessed the Sabbath day and made it holy.*[20] [Emphasis added.]

Rest is necessary for renewal and God ordained the Sabbath for our benefit.

Applications

While the Bible has much to say about the quality of work that must be done, it does not always give specific direction as to the type of work, profession, vocation, craft, or job that one should pursue. It is a difficult choice for young Christians who have just completed high school and are attempting to determine the proper training for their life's "tent making" occupation. Here, there are three primary activities which should be done. First, the person involved must determine, through prayer, what they are to do. The answer may not come in the form of a thundering voice from heaven but in a series of doors opening while other doors close. Also, it may occur over a number of years. God used 13 years (from age 17 to age 30) to get Jacob's son, Joseph, from the position of Potiphar's servant, and subsequently prisoner, to the "Prime Minister" of Egypt.[21] If one believes that *"the steps of a good man are ordered by the Lord: and he delighteth in his way."*[22] then one must conclude that the Lord is very active in employment decisions.

However, when one prays for a good crop, many believe that it should be done "with a hoe in hand" because God may act only after we have done what is humanly possible. Therefore, the second activity should be to assess talents and abilities through preference tests, ACT or SAT scores, grade point averages, or any other relevant tool that is available. Then, match those abilities with some honest employment.

Last, care must be given to distinguish between a vocation and an avocation. A vocation is a trade, business, profession, or occupation. On the other hand, an avocation is something that is done in addition to regular work or vocation. It is sometimes called a hobby. Some well-meaning people believe that they are preparing for a vocation when, in actuality, they discover that they are prepared for an avocation.

Also, one seeking new employment should monitor the supply and demand in employment fields and the projected future employment opportunities. At the same time, the _best_ people in any field generally can obtain employment directly related to their training. So, what might an avocation for some, may be a vocation for the best in the field. Therefore, one should diligently seek the position which allows that person to serve God most effectively.

Balancing Work and Family Responsibilities

Balancing work and family responsibilities is perhaps one of the most challenging tasks that a dedicated Christian must face today. If that balance is lost, then there can be detrimental consequences. Some men become "married" to their work by trying to do the best job possible in accordance with the Biblical admonition to do everything as if it were being done for the Lord. What are some Biblical guidelines for proper balance?

In the Old Testament miscellaneous laws, Moses, under the guidance of the Holy Spirit, wrote the following:

> _If a man has recently married, he must not be sent to war or have any other duty laid on him. For one year, he is to be free to stay at home and bring happiness to the wife he has married._[23]

While that may have had good practical application for the children of Israel at that time in their history, it would be very challenging to apply now. However, we should interpret this admonition as a very important principle for today—_family priorities are critical and deserve the highest emphasis._

When a job requires "marriage" to it, then it could be an indication that God has something else in mind for the worker. God could be closing that door and be in the process of opening another one for the worker. With work modification, another possibility is that the employment position could be done more effectively or efficiently by spending less time on the job. That, in turn, would allow more time to be spent on family activities. Through prayer and discussion with trusted counselors, the balance between work and family responsibilities can be achieved.

Chapter Summary

One must perform his job as if he were doing it for the Lord. Laziness, complaining, or other qualities which demonstrate less than total commitment to the job are not in accordance with the Word of God.

Any honest job is acceptable as shown by the large variety of jobs that God's people have had. In preparing for life's work, one should guard against preparing for an avocation rather than a vocation.

Time is money. Therefore, it should be utilized very carefully. Also, proper timing is important.

Because of the hard work of Christians, they have a built-in tendency to progress and be promoted in the working arena. In addition, the world of commerce provides an opportunity for ministry and Christian witness.

Chapter 5

DEBT AND CREDIT: BLESSING OR BANKRUPTCY?

"Let no debt <u>remain</u> outstanding, except the continuing debt to love one another…" **Romans 13:8 (NIV) [Emphasis added.]**

"Good will come to him who is generous and lends freely, who conducts his affairs with justice." **Psalm 112:5 (NIV)**

"The rich rule over the poor, and the borrower is servant to the lender." **Proverbs 22:7 (NIV)**

We are indebted. We are indebted to Christ for paying the price for our salvation with his own blood. We are indebted to our parents and others for early basic training. We owe a debt of gratitude to those who taught us to read or to enjoy many of the other skills that we possess. Many are indebted financially. Therefore, understanding debt is desirable. Improper use of debt can provide a living, haunting nightmare. However, many pitfalls of debt can be completely avoided by knowing and applying what the Bible teaches concerning debt (and spending). Praise God!

The Relationship Between Debt and Spending

What is the source of almost all debt challenges? The answer is ***spending***. Without acquiring assets or incurring expenses, there can be no debt which is owed. Effective spending will be covered in the next chapter.

CONTEMPORARY CHARACTERISTICS OF DEBT

Detrimental Aspects of Debt

The amount of debt in the U. S. is a staggering figure. According to the U. S. Federal Reserve Board's Web Site, ***revolving credit***, as of June, 2004, was $742,946,550,000. Other web sites estimate consumer debt in excess of $2 trillion or *$2,000,000,000,000*! What is even more incredible is the recent history of revolving credit as shown in Table 4-1.

Table 4-1
U. S. Revolving Credit Outstanding
U. S. Federal Reserve Board
(Total in $ millions)

January, 1968 (earliest month available)	$ 1,401.00
June, 1974	$ 12,138.00
June, 1984	$ 88,387.00
June, 1994	$331,247.00
June, 2004	$742,946.55

Source: U. S. Federal Reserve Board Web Site (www.federalreserve.gov/releases)

Table 4-1 indicates that, in less than 40 years, revolving credit as of June, 2004 has gone up _over 530 times_ what it was in January, 1968. The phrase "deferred gratification" seems to have vanished from the American way of life. From June, 1984 to June, 1994, revolving credit went up almost four times the June, 1984 amount. Finally, it more than doubled from June, 1994 to June, 2004. Some people have "hocked" their soul for worldly trinkets.

Another way of viewing the challenge facing our nation is to consider the "per person" amount. By dividing total revolving consumer credit outstanding by the population, we can see that the installment debt per person is approximately $2,857. That figure is even more astounding when we acknowledge that this includes every man, woman, and child ranging in age from new-born through 100 plus. Also, many owe nothing. Therefore, some have astronomical sums that they owe for declining value consumables. In addition, there are other forms of consumer debt besides revolving credit. When you look at the interest rate which is applicable on revolving credit, it could easily be renamed "revolting credit."

For some, debt becomes the equivalent of a narcotic and is habituating. It is crystal clear that some have stretched their credit line so thinly that the least financial reversal could break that line with a resounding *"snap"*. This perverse situation has the sickening label for some called "personal bankruptcy."

The statistics concerning consumer debt do not drive home the human suffering and anguish which may accompany financial difficulties. There are many factors which may contribute to the deterioration of a family. One of the straws which may "break the camel's back" is the straw of financial adversity. Children from broken homes often pay an enormous emotional price. All of which may be traced to the acquisition of *things* without the means of repayment. Quite clearly, consumer debt is a very serious challenge in the U.S. and one which no Christian should disregard. With this somber background on the detrimental aspects of debt, let us review some of the beneficial aspects of debt.

Beneficial Uses of Debt

James, the half-brother of Jesus, claims that from the *"same mouth come both blessing and cursing."* [1] While the detrimental aspects of debt have already been covered, there are some advantages which may accrue from incurring liabilities. However, most benefits result from acquiring capital or investment assets as opposed to consumables. Capital assets last for a relatively long period of time and may have the opportunity for appreciation in value. On the other hand, consumables last for a relatively short time and generally deteriorate to a point of virtual worthlessness. Moreover, **inflation** may work to the debtor's advantage and the creditor's detriment. The reason for the advantage is that the debtor repays the debt with dollars which have gone down in purchasing power while the underlying asset typically increases in value because of inflation. However, if our nation enters a period of deflation (instead of inflation), we could see the situation reversed.

For example, a home costing $90,000 ten years ago was acquired with a mortgage of $80,000 and a down-payment $10,000. If it has appreciated to a $200,000 fair market value today, then inflation (and market forces) have worked to the debtor's advantage because the mortgage can be paid off with dollars that are worth less than those dollars which were received when the mortgage was originated. By incurring debt, the buyer is $110,000 better off ($200,000 - $90,000) than the person would have been if no debt were incurred. This example shows how debt can have beneficial aspects.

Furthermore, most home owners would never have been able to buy a home if it were not for O.P.M. (other people's money). This illustration will be amplified in the chapter on housing and shelter. Also, many church facilities are financed. Therefore, when acquired judiciously, *some debts* may be beneficial.

DEBT AND THE BIBLE

In Shakespeare's play, <u>Hamlet</u>, Polonius advised: *"Neither a borrower nor a lender be."* [2] While the Bible does not directly support that line from the play, it does have adequate coverage concerning debt and credit.

Borrowing

Many fine Christians actually believe that Polonius was correct concerning borrowing. They base that belief on Romans 13:8 which states:

"Owe no man anything..." (KJV)

Actually, according to Greek language experts, the King James translation does not have the clearest modern translation. The New International Version of the Bible translates the same passage as:

"Let no debt remain outstanding..." (NIV)

The Revised English Bible states: *"Leave no debt outstanding..."* (REB)

There is a significant connotational difference between both the NIV and REB translations and the KJV translation. The KJV could be interpreted to mean that no debt is acceptable. While both NIV and REB indicate that the debt should be paid off in accordance with the terms of the agreement, they do not indicate that no debt should be incurred.

Again, debt is a two-edged sword. If used properly, debt can be beneficial. However, when abused, it can "cut to the quick" in a hurry.

Another reference to borrowing states: *"The wicked borrow and do not repay; but the righteous give generously."* [3] That passage should be a warning about lending money improperly.

As a caution concerning borrowing, Solomon declares: *"The poor are always ruled over by the rich, so don't borrow and put yourself under their power."* [4] This is one of many admonitions concerning the perils of borrowing.

In the Old Testament, God used the prophet Elisha and a miracle to drive home the dangers of debt. In II Kings 4:1-7, one of the upright men from the company of prophets died. When he died, he had an unpaid creditor who was going to take the widow's two sons to satisfy the debt. When Elisha asked what she had, she replied that she had a little oil. Elisha then told her to ask for all of her neighbor's empty jars that she could get. After she had done that, she closed her doors and began to pour the little bit of oil into all of the empty jars. When the last jar was filled, the oil stopped flowing.

Verse 7 of the passage states:

> She went and told the man of God, and he said, "Go, sell the oil and **pay your debts.** You and your sons can live off what is left." (NIV) [Emphasis added]

That Old Testament section provides another example of the dangers of debt.

Lending

While Polonius may have had a kernel of truth in his admonition against borrowing, his advice on lending does not square with the Bible. In numerous locations of the Word, God's people are told to be prepared to lend or, in some cases, to give. For example, Christ declared in the "Sermon on the Mount," that we are to: *"Give to anyone who asks; and do not turn your back on anyone who wants to borrow."* [5]

Again, in Luke, we are advised: *"But love your enemies, and do good, and **lend**, expecting nothing in return..."*[6] [Emphasis added.] In Psalms, David wrote: *"Good will come to him who is generous and lends freely, who conducts his affairs with justice."*[7] Also, in the Psalms, we have the following beautiful passage:

> *I was young and now I am old, yet I have never seen the righteous forsaken or their children begging bread. They are always generous and lend freely...*[8]

From these passages in both the Old and the New Testaments, it is clear that we are encouraged to lend <u>*with discretion*</u>.

As God's chosen people, the children of Israel were given strict ordinances concerning lending and borrowing. In Deuteronomy, God's inspired writer, Moses, told them:

> *For the Lord your God will bless you as he has promised, and you will lend to many nations but will borrow from none. You will rule over many nations but none will rule over you.*[9]

While the Israelites were forbidden from borrowing from foreign nations, they could borrow from each other. In Exodus, they were told:

> *"If you lend money to one of my people among you who is needy, do not be like a money lender; charge him no interest."*[10]

That passage did not mean that they were prevented from borrowing. On the contrary, they were told to borrow from each other but not from strangers. Therefore, in today's contemporary environment, Christians might consider borrowing from other Christians where feasible.

Interest on Money Loaned

In the Old Testament, the children of Israel were not allowed to charge interest to each other but they could charge foreigners:

> *You shall not charge interest to your countrymen: interest on money, food, or anything that may be loaned at interest. You may charge interest to a foreigner, but to your countryman you shall not charge interest, so that the Lord your God may bless you in*

all that you undertake in the land which you are about to enter to possess. [11]

On the other hand, a reasonable rate of interest is acceptable and expected in the New Testament. The parable of the talents—*"Then you ought to put my money in the bank, and on my arrival I would have received my money back with interest."* [12] –indicates that we can anticipate a fair return for money loaned. Therefore, appropriate interest charged or earned is in line with Biblical precepts today.

Credit

In order to obtain personal financing, you must have an acceptable credit rating. Simply stated, you must retire obligations in accordance with the stated terms of the related contracts in order to maintain a desirable credit report. In discussing the prerequisite for a good credit record, the Bible states:

"A good name is more desirable than great riches..." [13]

Eugene Peterson paraphrases that verse to say:

"A sterling reputation is better than striking it rich."

Along the same line, the writer of Ecclesiastes advised

"A good name is better than fine perfume..." [14]

Because Christians become people of integrity, honesty, and a good reputation, they should have no difficulty earning a good credit rating. However, a credit rating may have one of the same characteristics of a mirror. If a mirror is ever broken, it is difficult, if not impossible, to repair it. Likewise, if a person's credit rating is ever broken, that person will become suspect and may not enjoy unblemished credit for future transactions.

APPLICATIONS

Actually, by applying a good financial game plan (FGP), unnecessary debt may be eliminated by taking excess available cash and paying down consumer debts until they are fully paid. By forcing consumer (non-investment) expenditures always to be equal to or less than available cash, consumer debt will fade away like the morning dew on the grass when the sun hits it. ***HALLELUJAH!!*** **Praise the Lord.**

Closely tied to the FGP is the individual's spending habit. Disciplined modifications of spending addictions (covered in Chapter 6) will reduce or eliminate "impulse buying" and other poor spending policies. In turn, money which is not spent may be utilized to increase Christian giving, to reduce consumer debt, save for a "rainy day," or provide funds for investment. God's Holy Spirit will provide guidance for the appropriate decision. Therefore, financial planning and proper spending may eradicate consumer debt.

The Bible states that we should be content with only two things—food and raiment:

"if we have food and clothing let us rest content." [15]

However, too many Christians feel that they should have the biggest SUV (a kissing cousin to a Sherman Tank), latest gadget, and fanciest gizmo whether or not they have the necessary funds with which to buy those items. It is at that point that many well-meaning Christians sink into financial depression. To overcome those whims, there are strategies which allow financial stability and, at the same time, an enjoyable standard of living.

Credit Policy Statement #1

AVOID BUYING CONSUMER GOODS ON CREDIT.

Items which are personal in nature, and declining in value, should not be purchased on credit. This includes automobiles, television sets, and other consumer goods (non-investment purchases). The reason for that policy is that many consumer goods are going down in value at a faster rate than the reduction of debt associated with the asset. For example, a $20,000 automobile purchased primarily with debt may subsequently be worth only $14,000 while the related debt might be $15,500 or more. Therefore, a sale of the asset would not satisfy the debt with the proceeds from the sale.

Additionally, God has *promised* to supply our consumer needs:

*"And my God will supply **all** of your **needs** out of the **magnificence** of his riches in Christ Jesus"* [16] [Emphasis added.]

That is one of the most wonderful promises that we have from Our Father and His Son. When we buy consumer "goods" with debt, we take one of the "o's" out of goods and they become consumer "gods" or idols. God may have a different timetable from ours for supplying our consumer goods to us; when we jump ahead of Him with debt, we may usurp His judgment and fail to receive the full blessing He has in store for us from the purchased item. Further amplification on available purchasing alternatives is covered in Chapter 6.

Credit Policy Statement #2

IF MONTHLY CHARGE ACCOUNTS ENTICE YOU TO SPEND MORE THAN YOU CAN AFFORD, USE CASH ONLY INSTEAD OF CHARGE ACCOUNTS.

Charge accounts and credit cards may seduce people into making unwise purchases. If you become entrapped by that lust, perform "plastic surgery." Notify all creditors that you want to terminate all lines of credit. Then, take a pair of scissors and cut credit cards until they are unusable. A cash only plan will provide the catalyst for many to kick the overextended credit predicament.

On the other hand, elimination of charge accounts and credit cards is not necessary for everyone. There are many who can use credit cards as if they were spending cash and not abuse the credit privilege. With a credit card, there are certain advantages. First, you do not have to carry substantial sums of cash. In that way, losses caused by theft or negligence are minimized.

Second, you may use other people's money and earn interest with no marginal cost to you. For example, if you have an average of $1000 due per month in your credit card account, and you pay it off during the "grace period" before any charges or interest accrues, then you actually have a $1000 more to invest. If you are earning 5% on your money, then you will earn $50 more per year on your investments. Moreover, there are no annual charges or other charges of any kind for many bank credit cards if the bill is paid within the monthly "grace" billing period.

Furthermore, U.S. law generally prevents the consumer from paying more than $50 for unauthorized use of a card. (Incidentally, this charge may be waived in some instances.) If the card is reported missing before any charges are made on it, there is no liability for unauthorized charges. Therefore, for some (those who control its use), a credit card can be quite beneficial with no marginal costs to the user.

Credit Policy Statement #3

IN A PERIOD OF INFLATION, DEBT ACQUIRED FOR INVESTMENT ASSETS MAY PROVIDE REAL ECONOMIC BENEFITS.

Today, many people have their investments in the form of monetary assets. (Monetary assets are defined as checking accounts, savings accounts, money market funds and other money-equivalent assets.) However, inflation erodes the purchasing-power of monetary assets. For example, if you have funds in a 3% passbook-type savings account, you earn $3 for each $100 in the account. If the inflation rate is 4%, then the decrease in purchasing-power is $4. At the same time, the $3 interest income is subject to income taxes. In a 50% total tax bracket, the after-tax return would be $1.50. Therefore, in this illustration, you lose $4 in purchasing-power and gain $1.50 after taxes for a net loss of $2.50 for each $100. Obviously, if the tax rate or the inflation rate changes, the net loss would be different. However, the same general concept still applies.

To avoid the problem of encountering a real net loss in purchasing-power during a period of inflation, you may invest a portion of your assets in appreciating investments. The most logical investment for most people has been their personal residence. If future appreciation continues as it has in the past, then residences may prove to be a good inflation hedge. **(Obviously there are no guarantees and the housing market can go through periods of decline and correction just like the stock market did in 1999.) In fact, the housing market tumbled down in 2006 and has remained weak in many areas since that time.**

To illustrate the benefits of residential housing investment, on November 8, 1977, our family bought a personal residence in Norman, Oklahoma, paying $45,900 for it. Nine months later, the house sold for $53,398. In less than one year, the annual rate of return on the original investment was 21.79 % and the annual rate of return on the down-payment was 108.91%. Because of the tax laws that were in effect at that time, none of the gain was subject to tax. Obviously, the rate of return was far better than most investment alternatives and our family enjoyed the investment while we owned it.

INFLATION AND DEBT

There are many factors which tend to fuel inflation including, but not limited to:
1. Global fuel prices
2. Deficit government spending
3. Under-funded social programs
4. Corporate greed
5. Individual avarice

Therefore, in the absence of a total collapse, inflation is likely to continue in the U.S. This, in turn, reinforces the position that debt for capital or investment assets may provide significant financial benefits to debtors at the expense of creditors.

THE 5 C's OF CREDIT

Bankers often essentially use 5 C's for credit evaluation. It is primarily for the protection of the lender. However, it is also a protection for borrowers as well. The 5 C's are:
1 Character
2 Capacity
3 Collateral
4 Capital
5 Conditions to evaluate potential debtors

As a guideline for _borrowers_, any proposed debt should be evaluated carefully before the debt is incurred. If any one of the 5 C's guidelines cannot be satisfied, the debt should probably not be undertaken even if the lender is willing to make the loan.

First, the potential borrower should have a good character. The individual should be a person of integrity and have a reputation for honest prior dealings. In short, all Christians should be above reproach on this guideline.

Next, the potential debtor should have capacity for repayment. Do current or future income levels provide funds for repayment? Does the investment generate a net cash-flow large enough for debt repayment? If the answer to those, or similar questions, is negative, then the borrower may consider avoiding the debt.

Third, the collateral for the debt should be scrutinized. If it has the potential to decrease in value, then it may be a questionable expenditure. On the other hand, potential appreciation of the asset may make it a desirable investment.

The fourth item to be considered is the capital of the potential debtor. In this context, capital is the difference between total assets and total debts. As a general statement, the larger the person's capital, the safer the debt. However, persons with small capital may have the greatest need for borrowing. Therefore, the other four C's may be considered apart from capital in some situations.

The last C, conditions, should be evaluated before any debt is incurred. For example, if a corporate retrenchment is known to be imminent and a person's job were threatened, then the debt might be placed in abeyance until economic conditions improve.

Facetiously, some claim that the only people who can qualify for loans are those who do not need them. By applying the 5 C's, that may appear true. However, consumer debt restraint generally will be beneficial to both the lender and the borrower.

Chapter Summary

Debt is potentially a very dangerous two-edged sword. When utilized prudently and with serious planning, it can be beneficial and allow equity to increase. However, when it is used carelessly and improperly, it may be a terrible train wreck coming down the track. Treat debt the same way that you would treat a loaded machine gun around young children—very, very, carefully.

With proper respect, debt can be a good friend. However, when debt is handled frivolously, it can be your worst nightmare. ***Always be very careful with debt.***

CHAPTER 6

SPENDING WISELY—MONEY MANAGEMENT IN ACTION: LIVING WITHIN YOUR MEANS

"Why spend your money for what is not food, your earnings on what fails to satisfy?
Listen to me and you will fare well, you will enjoy the fat of the land."
Isaiah 55:2 (NEB)

"Don't be obsessed with getting more material things.
Be relaxed with what you have. Since God has assured us,
'I'll never let you down, never walk off and leave you,' ... " **Hebrews 13:5 (TM)**

Previously, we have observed that "personal equity" can be increased only by increasing revenues while holding expenses constant or by decreasing expenses while holding revenues constant. A third possibility is to do both simultaneously; raise revenues and decrease expenses. Because expense management is so critical to personal financial success, it is desirable to master policies and techniques that will bridle any tendencies to "overspend."

Eugene Peterson expresses I Timothy 6:8 to read:

> *"Since we entered this world penniless and will leave it penniless,*
> *if we have bread on the table and shoes on our feet, that's enough."*
> (TM)

After we have been blessed with essential "food and raiment," any additional expenditures should be handled with great thought, care, and analysis. At a very early age, my maternal granddad used to tell me: "Clyde, if you will watch your pennies, the dollars will take care of themselves." At that time, a penny had some value and many candies cost only a *penny*. An application for the U.S. Government might be that if they would watch their millions, then the billions and trillions would take care of themselves. The point is clear. If expenditures at the lowest level are monitored carefully, then the higher levels will automatically be in line with our objectives. Unfortunately, many people and institutions do not know how to spend wisely. Some, on the other hand know how to spend, but, for whatever reason, don't do it.

"Keeping Up With the Joneses"

One of the worst mistakes that can be made is to try and "keep up with the Joneses." A friend of mine puts it like this:

"Some people buy things they don't want with money they don't have to impress neighbors they don't like."

No philosophy could be more irrational. Yet, we witness it every day.

God's Word takes an entirely different point-of-view. Paul declared:

*"I am not saying this because I am in need, for I have **learned** to be content whatever the circumstances."* [1] [Emphasis added.]

The writer of Hebrews admonished:

Let your way of life be free from the love of money, being content with what you have; for He Himself has said, "I will never desert you, nor will I ever forsake you." [2]

King David said:

"But as for me, my contentment is not in wealth but in seeing you and knowing all is well between us. And when I awake in heaven, I will be fully satisfied, for I will see you face to face. [3]

Haggai lamented:

"You have planted much, but have harvested little. You eat, but never have enough. You drink but never have your fill. You put

on clothes, but are not warm. You earn wages, only to put them in a purse with holes in it." [4]

In all of the references above, the appropriate point is that contentment does not consist of buying and having things, but, to enjoy a warm relationship with the Lord. The antithesis of Christian living is the covetous philosophy of trying to "keep up with the Joneses."

Christians' Priorities in Spending

The proper Christian philosophy is found in Christ's own words when he said:

"But seek first his kingdom and his righteousness, and all of these shall be yours as well." [5]

When we spend our money, we need to do it in a systematic and prioritized fashion. *First,* we need to return to God the appropriate amount with the right attitude in order to "seek first his kingdom" and to affirm his Lordship and divine provision for our lives. After that, basic living essentials—including food, clothing, and shelter—will be covered. A Biblical guideline is to tithe 10% to God and save 10% as well. The remaining 80% is where great thought, care, and analysis come into play. Table 3-1 on p. 27 provides guidelines for spending. If a Christian's revenues are not going up, then spending is generally the only variable that can be changed for financial stability.

Biblical Principles for Spending

A drop of water is a relatively small amount. However, a faucet that drips only one drop of water every two seconds will leak a gallon in short order and many gallons over weeks and months. So it is with spending. Many small items each day add up to an extremely large amount in a matter of weeks. One key to successful spending is to plug those small cash leaks and not let them redevelop. The Bible has many principles that are applicable for management of spending. Several parables, stories, and other illustrations do not have their primary emphasis in the area of spending but may be applied in that way.

Pearl Buying

For example, Jesus related a parable of a jewel merchant who dealt in pearls.

> *"Again, the kingdom of heaven is like a merchant looking for fine pearls. When he found one of great value, he went away and sold everything he had and bought it."* [6]

While the principal teaching of the parable is that heaven is worth everything that we have in this life, including life itself, the parable also has application for spending. The merchant was "looking for fine pearls." In other words, the merchant was "shopping." He compared the price and quality of pearls of one seller with the price and quality of other sellers. Also, he may have compared service during the sale and service after the sale. In short, he was making all of the rational decisions that go into a wise purchase. When making purchases, we should engage in a similar type of activity.

Fraudulent Sales = Disappointing Purchases

The Bible covers a number of fraudulent activities that are still practiced today. In dealing with the nation of Israel through the prophet Amos, God proclaimed:

> *Listen to this, you that grind the poor and suppress the humble in the land while you say, 'When will the new moon be over so that we may sell grain? When will the Sabbath be past so that we may expose our wheat for sale, giving short measure in the bushel and taking overweight in the silver, tilting the scales fraudulently, and selling the refuse of the wheat; that we may buy the weak for silver and the poor for a pair of sandals?* [7]

We need to be on guard to avoid merchants and craftsmen who are engaged in any type of shady dealings by selling the "refuse of the wheat" and patronize those operating with integrity and ethical standards. "An ounce of prevention is worth a pound of cure."

Family Instruction

In Proverbs, Solomon declared:

"Train a child in the way he should go, and when he is old he will not turn from it."[8]

A chain is as strong as its weakest link. Therefore, if anyone in the family is an untrained spender, family training sessions should be initiated to reinforce the proper type of spending.

Impulse Buying

There is a body of research which indicates that, in some instances, buying is done impulsively or on a whim by the purchaser. In the Bible, two kings made decisions impulsively and later regretted their decisions. In the first instance, when the children of Israel were in captivity in Babylon, Darius was elevated to the position of king according to Daniel 5:30. He then appointed 120 governors to rule throughout the kingdom, with three administrators over them, one of whom was Daniel. Because Daniel was held in such high esteem and performed his duties so well, the jealous governors could find no grounds for charges against him.

At that point, the governors set out to trap Daniel. Then, they persuaded King Darius to establish a law that anyone who prayed within a thirty day period to any god or man, except the king, should be thrown into the lion's den. When Daniel knew that the decree had been published, he went home to his upstairs room and prayed three times a day, as he had in the past, in full view of the governors who were watching. Immediately, of course, the governors brought that information to the king. When the king realized that he had been duped and that he was going to have to throw Daniel into the lion's den, the king *"was sore displeased with himself."*[9] The king acted impulsively and lived to regret it. Through God's divine intervention, an angel shut the lions' mouths and Daniel was unhurt.

In the second episode, King Herod acted very impetuously and impulsively. Because of a smoldering grudge that Herod's wife, Herodias, had against John the Baptist, she looked for the appropriate time to vent her anger and get even with John. Finally, the opportune time came. When King Herod had his birthday banquet, he invited all of the "movers and shakers" of Galilee to the gala affair. A portion of the festivities included a dance routine by the daughter of Herodias. That dance so beguiled the king and charmed his guests that the king lost all sense of perspective and common sense.

The following conclusion to the matter is recorded in the gospel of Mark:

> *The king said to the girl, "Ask me for anything you want and I'll give it to you." And he promised with an oath, "Whatever you ask I will give you, up to half of my kingdom." She went out and said to her mother, "What shall I ask for?" "The head of John the Baptist," she answered. At once the girl hurried in to the king with the request: "I want you to give me right now the head of John the Baptist on a platter."* [10]

The king realized immediately that he had become a fool. But, because of the oath and his dinner guests, the king granted the request.

In both of the above actions by King Darius and King Herod, there was regret over their folly because of their rash impulsive choices. Is it possible, to a much lesser degree, that when we purchase items impulsively and without the proper analysis of the purchase, we may suffer grief and could experience a condition known as "buyer's remorse." Both of the kings felt great distress as a result of their impetuous decisions. Impulsive decisions may provide remorse whether it involves spending or other areas of life. It is clear that we should generally guard against impulse purchases.

On the other hand, when we have been looking for and evaluating a specific purchase for some time, without success, and we subsequently find the exact item at the right price, we may need to take advantage of it immediately before someone else does. Real estate purchases may be a good example.

Timing

In discussing the benefits of advance preparation, Solomon used the ant as an example:

Go to the ant, you sluggard, observe her ways and gain wisdom. She has no prince, no governor or ruler; but in summer she gathers in her store of food and lays in her supplies at harvest.[11]

As the ant provides for winter needs during the summer, so can consumers. Seasonal goods or services purchased *out of season* may provide the greatest value. It is the same idea as buying a straw hat in the middle of winter or other seasonal clothing at the end of a season. You may observe other areas where timing is important.

"Ready Funds"

For some, true bargains or unforeseen crises come after all funds have been spent. The prodigal son discovered that predicament after he wasted his substance on riotous living.

"After he had spent everything, there was a severe famine in that whole country, and he began to be in need." [12] [Emphasis added.]

Because emergencies or outstanding buys may develop unannounced, it is desirable to have a cash reserve available for special situations. The exact amount will vary from family to family, but a three-month cushion will provide additional peace of mind.

Astute Bargaining

Astute bargaining and negotiating go all the way back to Genesis. Perhaps the most interesting bargaining session in the history of world was conducted between *God and Abraham*. Yes, that's right—God and Abraham. In the 18th chapter of Genesis, Abraham negotiated with God for the citizens of Sodom. According to God's Word, Abraham initiated the negotiations by asking God if He would spare the city if 50 righteous people could be found. In Genesis 18:26, the Lord responded in the following way:

The Lord said, "If I find fifty righteous people in the city of Sodom, I will spare the whole place for their sake. (NIV)

The negotiations continued with Abraham decreasing the number consecutively from 50 to 10 in increments. Each time that Abraham made an offer; the offer was accepted by the Lord.

The negotiations were concluded in the following manner:

> *He answered, "For the sake of ten, I will not destroy it. When the Lord had finished speaking with Abraham, he left and Abraham returned home.* [Genesis 18:32a-33]

While the Lord accepted every offer by Abraham, Sodom never qualified, *even with only ten people,* and God annihilated the cities of Sodom and Gomorrah with burning sulfur ("fire and brimstone").

What does this story have to do with spending? Actually, it illustrates the benefits of negotiations in obtaining the lowest price and presents some excellent negotiating tools. Many times, when I have felt that I have bargained for the lowest price for a proposed purchase, I have asked: "What is the lowest price that you would take for this item?" Sometimes, when the seller responds, it is with an even lower price than I was prepared to pay initially. Purchase prices can be significantly reduced many times through astute negotiating and bargaining.

Also, Solomon included bargaining in the Proverbs:

> *"Utterly worthless!" says the buyer as he haggles over the price. But afterwards he brags about the bargain!*[13]

Bargaining and negotiating are not comfortable for everyone. However, for those who relish the process, it can provide substantially lower prices and increased net personal equity.

The Spendthrift

The Living Bible describes the spendthrift in the following way:

> *"The wise man saves for the future but the foolish man spends whatever he gets."*[14]

The New English Bible translates the same verse as:

> *"The wise man has a houseful of fine and costly treasures; the stupid man will fritter them away."*[15]

Over and over, the Bible censures unnecessary spending and wastage. At the same time, saving, but not in a miserly and selfish way, is encouraged.

Sabbath Buying

There are six days per week set aside for work and other pursuits. In the Old Testament, the seventh day was set aside for worship and rest. In observing the Lord's commands, regulations, and decrees during the rebuilding of the Jerusalem wall in Nehemiah's day, the workers agreed:

> *"When the neighboring peoples bring merchandise or grain to sell on the Sabbath, we will not buy from them on the Sabbath or any holy day."*[16]

While the admonition is for the Sabbath, Christians generally worship and rest on the first day of the week in accordance with Acts 20:7 and other New Testament passages. While we are now under "grace" rather than "law," that guidance is still appropriate.

The Smartest Purchase

In chapter one, we evaluated the "perfect investment." Now, we want to appraise the "perfect purchase." Solomon proclaimed:

> *"Buy the **truth** and do not sell it; get wisdom, discipline and understanding."*[17] [Emphasis added.]

Jesus stated strongly:

> *"…I am the way, and the **truth** and the life. No one comes to the Father except through me."*[18] [Emphasis added.]

Actually, when we "buy the truth," we receive Jesus and His sacrifice as a free gift. To *"buy the **truth**"* is the best purchase that we can ever make.

The Blank Check

As we have discussed previously, God has given us a great "blank check" for spending in Philippians 4:19. Here, it states:

*"And my God **will** meet all of your **needs** according to his glorious riches in Christ Jesus."* [19] [Emphasis added.]

It is reassuring to know that God <u>already</u> knows what we need even before we ask. He is going to fulfill all of our true <u>needs</u>.

Summary

Wise spending can be summarized with the following adage:
If your *out-go* exceeds your *income*, it will be your *down fall.*

While it <u>seems</u> easy enough to control spending and to live within one's means, for many, the application is quite difficult. However, with discipline, careful monitoring, and determination, it can be done. In addition, God knows our true needs and has promised to meet those needs. We must operate on faith many times and believe that He will do what He has said that He will do.

Practical Application of Spending Principles

The following "check list" may help in applying the Biblical concepts that have been discussed:

1. Is there a genuine need for this product or service?
2. Will this product or service meet my need?
3. Is this the "best" price that I can get for this product or service?
4. Is there a better time to buy the product or service?
5. If this item has been discounted, is it "obsolete" or superseded?
6. If the item has been advertised as "on sale," is it really a sale price?
7. Are there other items which could be substituted?
8. Are there any unacceptable disadvantages associated with this product?
9. If this is a "luxury" item, would a "lesser" product suffice?
10. If this a "lower line" product, would a higher priced line meet my needs better over the long-run?

11. Have I done my "home work" and analyzed this product adequately?
12. Does the seller "stand behind the product"?
13. Are there local services that should be provided with this product?

If all of the answers to the questions are satisfactory, then wait at least 24 hours for a major expenditure and "sleep on the purchase" before consummating it. You will be surprised at how many times you will avoid making a "bad decision." If you subsequently close the deal, then you will have the peace of mind of knowing that you have made an "optimal" buy and will enjoy the product or service even more.

At first, this may seem like an "ordeal." However, by practicing those principles for a while, they generally will become internalized and be a very valuable tool for spending procedures.

Chapter Summary

Because of advertising, the media, peer pressure, and other forces, we are constantly bombarded with the message: "You can have everything and you can have it now." However, that message is in direct contradiction with economic reality for almost all of us. My mother used to say that many couples want to start their marriage where your Father and I hoped to be after working for 50 years. Unfortunately, as a general statement, we are a nation of "buy now and pay later." That philosophy has gotten a large segment of our society into great difficulty and financial ruin.

But, it does not have to be that way. By carefully monitoring expenditures and expenses, we can overcome that tendency and have a life-style that is well within our means. If you are not already doing that, make a prayerful commitment to do so today.

CHAPTER 7

HOUSING AND SHELTER:
"UNLESS THE LORD BUILDS THE HOUSE,
ITS BUILDERS LABOR IN VAIN."

"Unless the Lord builds a house, the builders' work is useless."
Psalm 127:1a (LB)

"There is plenty of room for you in my Father's home."
John 14:2a (TM)

The Need for Shelter

Through the ages, mankind has needed shelter. From Genesis to Revelation, man has sought earthly shelter and a heavenly home. Noah needed shelter from the great flood and built an ark.[1] Mary and Joseph found no shelter for them in the inn and had to lay Jesus in a manger.[2] Jesus used a house for the last supper.[3] That same need for shelter continues to the present time.

There have been Scriptural examples where God's people had only temporary shelter. Even Jesus did not have a home on earth and revealed:

"...Foxes have holes, and birds of the air have nests; but the Son of man has nowhere to lay his head."[4]

When Jesus sent his disciples out in pairs, they were instructed to take nothing except for a staff. Also, they were told, *"Where you enter a house, stay there until you leave the place."* [5] Therefore, those of us with homes should be extremely thankful and realize that we have received something that Christ and his disciples did not always enjoy. Let's examine what the Bible has to offer concerning housing and shelter.

The Perfect Home

Christians already have the perfect home but they have not taken possession of it yet. Jesus said:

> *"There are many homes up there where my Father lives, and I am going to prepare them for your coming."* [6]

In describing the "new Jerusalem" in heaven, John portrays the city in the following way:

> *"The twelve gates were twelve pearls, each gate made of a single pearl. The great street of the city was of pure gold, like transparent glass"* [7]

To make it even more exciting and interesting, Isaiah boldly proclaims:

> *"Then the wolf will live with the lamb, and the leopard lie down with the kid; the calf and the young lion will feed together, with a little child to tend them."* [8]

It is very obvious from the above discussion that our finite understanding of what an Infinite God has prepared for us is beyond our full comprehension. One thing is certain, however; our heavenly home will make any home on earth look like a chicken wire and cardboard box lean-to. I am anxious to see what mine looks like; aren't you?

While the Christian has a home in heaven, it is necessary to have shelter on the earth. The King James Version describes our heavenly home poetically in the "Pastoral Discourse" where Christ said:

> *"In my Father's house are many mansions: if it were not so, I would have told you. I go to prepare a place for you, and if I go*

and prepare a place for you, I will come again and receive you unto myself; that where I am, <u>there ye may be also.</u>" [9] [Emphasis added.]

It is interesting to note that Paul's letter to Timothy states:

"But if we have food and clothing, we will be content with that." [10]

Nothing specifically is mentioned about shelter. However, the "great blank check" – Philippians 4:19 states: "But my God shall supply all your need according to his riches in glory by Christ Jesus."

Therefore, if shelter is a need, our God will supply it just as he did for Mary and Joseph in the stable.

Earthly Shelter and the Bible

We know that:

"Every good and perfect gift is from above, coming down from the Father of the heavenly lights, who does not change like shifting shadows." [11]

Therefore, good shelter comes from the Lord and we should dedicate our dwelling place to the furtherance of His kingdom just as Solomon consecrated the temple in I Kings chapter 8 and Nehemiah dedicated the newly rebuilt wall in Nehemiah chapter 12.

The belief that the Lord provides shelter, security, and food is borne out in Psalm 127. There, in a psalm attributed to Solomon, it states:

"Unless the Lord builds the house, its builders labor in vain." [12]

If the Lord is not involved with the shelter decision, then it will be a less than satisfactory experience. Perhaps that is why Solomon wrote:

"Better a dry crust with peace and quiet than a house full of feasting with strife." [13]

Could it be that Solomon's 700 hundred wives and 300 concubines made him an authority on that situation?

In addition to divine dedication, dwelling places should have a good foundation. That point was driven home by Jesus in the "Sermon on the Mount." There, Christ compared the wise man who built his house on the rock (Christ – the good foundation) with the foolish man who built his house on the sand (non-Christian living – the poor foundation). When the rains and winds came, the wise man's house withstood the test. On the other hand, the foolish man's house could not withstand the stormy blasts and fell in a tremendous crash.

Although the parable of the "Wise and Foolish Builders" was intended for a spiritual illustration, it is also true for physical shelter as well. The foundation for a home (both spiritual and physical) is extremely important. Failure to provide a good foundation can be disastrous as evidenced by past mud slides in California which have destroyed many expensive homes.

Selecting Shelter: Purchase or Rent?

Purchase?

It is my belief and experience that when we pray for God's Will in our lives, He will answer our petition in accordance with the following promise that Jesus described:

> *"And I will do whatever you ask **in my name**, so that the Son may bring glory to the Father."*[14] [Emphasis added.]

That same idea is accented <u>four additional times</u> in the gospel of John alone. (John 15:7, 15:16, 16:23-24). This wonderful promise is also stressed in Matthew 7:7, 21:22, Mark 11:24, Luke 11:9, James 1:5, I John 3:22, and 5:14. Does it seem reasonable that we can take that promise to the bank when it has been emphasized **twelve** times in the New Testament? God will open and shut doors to provide unexpected benefits when we are living our lives in the center of His Will and bringing honor and glory to Him.

When we pray for shelter, God will provide in accordance with His Will and His timetable. While homes may be received by gift or inheritance, most of us will have to face the decision of whether to buy or rent. It is interesting to note that in one case, the children of Israel were commanded to build houses. When they were exiled from Jerusalem to Babylon, God told the children of Israel through Jeremiah, the prophet:

"This is the text of the letter that the prophet Jeremiah sent from Jerusalem to the surviving elders among the exiles and to the priests, the prophets and all the other people Nebuchadnezzar had carried into exile from Jerusalem to Babylon. This is what the Lord Almighty, the God of Israel, says to all those I carried into exile from Jerusalem to Babylon: **Build houses** *and settle down; plant gardens and eat what they produce."* [15] [Emphasis added.]

While Nebuchadnezzar's yoke was oppressive and the exiles longed to leave their captivity, God sentenced them to seventy years under Babylonian bondage. However, they were to make the best of it. Moreover, they were told to build houses and sink some roots because they were going to be there for a long time.

From that history of the children of Israel, we can see that building a house may be desirable when Christians are expecting to remain in a location for a relatively long time. In today's society, building a house might also include buying a house. Generally, over a relatively long period of time, buying or building a home is an economic "slam dunk" over renting.

For example, I owned a beautiful 4 bedroom, 2 bath rental home in Ruston, Louisiana and was getting $795 rental revenue per month. When I decided to sell it, the purchasers obtained a mortgage with payments which were $200 lower than what they would have had to pay in rent for the same house. Their principal down-payment was very low because they were "first time home buyers." Now, they are building up equity in the home and will have something to sell if they decide to move. Ultimately, they will own the home outright with no debt when the mortgage is paid off.

What would they have had if they had "leased" rather than purchasing the property? At the end of the mortgage period, they would have had: (1) a box of worthless rental receipts, (2) nothing that they could sell, and (3) no equity in the property. Also, they would have had a greater cash outlay to lease the property than they will have to buy it.

Is a Home an Investment?

There are no guarantees associated with earthly investments. However, it is guaranteed that all investments will achieve one of three possibilities. An investment will **always**: (1) go up in value, (2) maintain the same value, or (3) go down in value. Housing is no exception to that rule.

However, over a number of years, housing has generally been a very conservative investment and has gone up in value. For many Christians, housing is the best investment that they make during their lifetime. **But,** there may be some housing markets which have been pushed up to such a high level, that those market bubbles could burst and go down in value.

The old adage of "investigate before you invest" is still good advice for potential housing investments. That investigation should be bathed in prayer and done as thoroughly and completely as possible. Also, to the extent that it can be done, all emotional aspects of home buying should be removed. Proverbs 11:22 (NIV) states:

"Plans fail for lack of counsel, but with many advisers they succeed."

When a person is not knowledgeable about a specific real estate market, good advice would be to seek counsel from those who are specialists in that geographic area in order to review and analyze alternatives.

While home ownership **_may_** be a wonderful investment, some other advantages of home ownership include: paying the mortgage off with dollars that are worth less than the dollars which were obtained at the:

1. time of the mortgage origination because of inflation,
2. the potential for income tax deductions for interest and property taxes on the property,
3. appreciation potential,
4. significant tax advantages for a profitable sale, and
5. general "pride of ownership."

Rent or Lease?

The word *rent* appears many times in Scripture and comes from the word *rend*. In most instances, the word *rent* refers to "tearing." An example is shown in Genesis 37:34:

"And Jacob rent his clothes and put sackcloth upon his loins, and mourned for his son for many days." [KJV]

It is obvious that Jacob tore his clothes.

In modern usage, the word *rent* generally means to have the legal use of property for a specified time period. In that context, the word *rent* is not found in the King James translation. However, the word *leasing* is found twice in Psalm 4:2 and 5:6. In each case, it means "falsehoods" or "lies." Because the words *rent* and *lease*, or variations, are not found in the Bible does that mean that it is silent on those topics?

Perhaps we can gain some insights from the Word of God on these terms by looking at the way that the disciples were sent out "two by two." In Mark 6:10 [NIV], it states:

"Whenever you enter a house, stay there until you leave that town."

In their journeys it was always possible that they would be in a location for a short time and then move on. The passage does not say that they were to build or buy a house while they were there. From the instructions given to the disciples, we might infer that it is alright to rent or lease when we believe that we will be in a place for a relatively short time. However, if the expected relatively short period of time turns into a relatively long period of time, then a re-evaluation might be in order.

U. S. Government Incentives

Income Tax Benefits

Income Tax Deductions

Congress has decided that home ownership is important and has provided certain incentives for home ownership in the U. S. Internal Revenue Code [IRC]. The IRC generally allows a deduction for home mortgage interest and property taxes when itemized deductions are taken. However, when the standard deduction is utilized, then there is no deduction for those expenses. In many instances, those two potential deductions will determine whether a person or couple itemizes or takes the standard deduction. In effect, the tax savings from home ownership deductions subsidize the homeowner but do not provide any benefit to the renter.

Excluded Tax-Free Income

In addition to potential deductions for mortgage interest and property taxes, homeowners can generally sell their homes and have up to $500,000 in gains excluded from taxable income. Like most provisions of the tax law, this provision can be very technical and complex. However, the general rule is that if a person or couple has lived in a principal residence for at least 2 years out of a 5 year period ending on the date of the sale, then they can sell the residence and not pay any income tax on a specified amount of the gain. The amount of tax-free gain for a single individual is $250,000 and $500,000 for a couple filing a joint return. In summary, there are specific U. S. income tax provisions designed to encourage home ownership.

Physical Characteristics

In the ten commandments, God told Moses, "Thou shalt not covet thy neighbor's house,…"[16] One way to apply that commandment is to ascertain the unique home needs of a person's family and obtain those needs without any wasted space. Bigger houses mean higher property taxes, insurance, and operating expenses. With energy costs at record levels, excess space to heat and cool is a liability rather than an asset. On the other side of the coin, a house that is cramped and uncomfortable for its occupants can be most disagreeable.

The physical characteristics of a house are all significant considerations. Yet, many people overlook obvious flaws in property because of their emotional involvement in home selection, haste in decision-making, or other unexplainable reasons.

Some of the major considerations are:

1. The surrounding neighborhood

One of the most important features in home ownership is the neighborhood. Some real estate experts believe that the three most important characteristics of real estate are: "location, location, and location." Is the property in line with other properties in the area? Is it close to a railroad grade crossing, an interstate highway, or some other annoying factor? Is the neighborhood in an ascending cycle or has it begun to decline? A thorough investigation into the neighborhood will pay big dividends and may make the difference between home enjoyment and "buyer's remorse."

2. The house itself

Is the floor-plan in accordance with your needs? Is the lot configuration really what you want? These questions, along with a host of others, make it desirable to have a check-list with all of the desired characteristics that you want in your home. In that way, some of the emotional aspects of the purchase are eliminated.

3. The appliances and other implements

Does the air-conditioning system operate properly? Are the appliances in good working order? In order to verify these questions, and many related items, it is generally desirable to have a "home inspector" inspect and evaluate everything in the home before it is purchased. The contract should generally have a clause for inspection and provide that all defective attributes will be corrected before closing or have the purchase price reduced to compensate for the deficiencies.
Other factors

The needs and desires for each person and family are different. Every home should be purchased to meet those unique needs and desires. King Solomon stated: "Wicked men are overthrown and are no more, but the house of the righteous stands firm."[17] The desire of every Christian is to have a home that stands firm and secure and one which brings honor and glory to the Lord. With prayer and careful planning, a home can achieve those goals.

Forced Savings

For some, saving is a very difficult task. However, purchasing a home provides a forced savings plan even in those instances when the value of the home remains the same as the purchase price or does not go up in value. The reason that one has forced savings is that some portion of each payment in the normal repayment schedule retires part of the mortgage obligation and increases one's equity in the home. As a result of that provision, many save without even realizing it.

Financial Guidelines for Purchase

When arranging for financing of homes it is necessary to "qualify." To "qualify," one must satisfy the criteria established by the financing agency or institution. While criteria will vary because of different economic conditions, intense competition in the mortgage industry because of the internet and other factors has spawned some questionable contracts. For example, interest-only mortgages for a specified time, such as two years, have made some believe that they can afford an expensive home when, in fact, they are in debt over their heads. However, when they must begin paying ***interest and amortize the principal***, they realize that the debt is too much. Precise projections concerning future cash-flow will generally help to avoid excessive debt. By necessity, there may be trade-offs between mortgage payments and other expenditures such as recreation or eating out.

In summary, you should obligate yourself with a mortgage only if you believe that God's Holy Spirit is leading you to go into debt in that way. If you have any reservations about the proposed liability, you should re-evaluate the decision and be absolutely certain that the transaction is the best option that you have available. Don't forget that King Solomon, the wealthiest man in his day, proclaimed:

> *The rich lord it over the poor; the borrower becomes the lender's slave*[18]

Incurring an ill-advised mortgage can force the borrower into slavery and become a draconian drag on your Christian witness.

Chapter Summary

Home ownership has provided many with their safest investment in recent years. However, there have been "bubbles" in the real estate market just like those in the stock market. Future appreciation for home ownership is not totally clear but the factors of limited supply and inflation, make it a good risk, but, a risk nevertheless.

Everyone has to have shelter. Over the long term, buying a home will generally be superior to renting. A good home can be an invaluable asset in one's Christian witness and ministry.

CHAPTER 8

INVESTMENTS AND WEALTH IN GENERAL— USING GOD'S RESOURCES TEMPORARILY FOR EARTHLY MINISTRY

Then you should have invested my money with the bankers, and at my coming I would have received what was my own with interest. Matthew 25:27 (AMP)

Investment Advisers

Because of the complexity of many fields, advisers are needed. When we have a medical problem, we generally seek a medical professional if we are not healed in a reasonable period of time. Legal challenges may require the advice of a competent attorney. Also, advice is usually needed when it comes to making investments.

The Bible confirms the need for investment advice in many different venues. In Proverbs 11:14, the NIV translation states:

For lack of guidance a nation falls, but many advisers make victory sure.

While this verse deals primarily with a nation at war, it is also applicable to investments. A little further in Proverbs 13:10 where it states:

Pride only breeds quarrels, but wisdom is found in those who take advice.

Advice is desirable to avoid contentions. With advice as a backdrop, let us turn our attention to investments.

Investments in General

It is interesting that the word "investment" or "investments" is not used in the King James Version of the Bible. However, the words: "gain", "gained", and "gains" are found with some frequency and are the "returns" on investments or labor in our current society. Making investments is not stressed nearly as much in God's Word as it is in our world today.

In fact, many times investments are reviewed negatively in the Bible. For example, when the rich young ruler approached Jesus and asked Him, "Good teacher, what must I do to inherit eternal life?" Ultimately, Jesus' response to the young ruler was:

> *You still lack one thing. Sell everything you have and give to the poor, and you will have treasure in heaven. Then come, follow me.*

> *When he heard this, he became very sad, because he was a man of great wealth.*

> *Jesus looked at him and said, "How hard is it for the rich to enter the kingdom of God! Indeed, it easier for a camel to go through the eye of a needle than for a rich man to enter the kingdom of God."* [1]

There has been much discussion about the advice given to the rich young ruler. Jesus is God and knew the heart of the young man. The fact that the young man asked, *"what must I do"* indicates that he may have felt that there were specific actions to be performed which would warrant the awarding of eternal life. He may not have understood that eternal life is a free gift that requires believing faith and a change of heart brought about by God's Holy Spirit.

By reading and meditating on the story of the rich young ruler, can we infer that wealth (the end result of savings and investment) is inherently evil? That conclusion is not always confirmed in the Word of God. As a prime example, Jesus was buried in the tomb of Joseph of Arimathea. In Matthew 27:57, the Bible states: "When it was evening, there came a rich man from Arimathea, named Joseph, who also was a disciple of Christ." (AMP) In that verse, there are two characteristics that are used to describe this man: (1) rich and (2) a disciple of Jesus. Because Joseph had both traits concurrently, they are not mutually exclusive. In effect, wealth, like money, is a neutral object. It can be used to start churches, to send missionaries, or for other beneficial Christian activities. However, it can also be used for sinful purposes as well. Wealthy people must make decisions concerning the utilization of their property—Is it going to be used for good or evil?

In another parable concerning wealth, Jesus described a rich fool. In Luke 12:16-21, Jesus indicted the foolish man in the following way:

> *The ground of a certain rich man produced a good crop. He thought to himself, 'What shall I do? I have no place to store my crops.'*

> *Then he said, 'This is what I'll do. I will tear down my barns and build bigger ones, and there I will store all of my grain and my goods. And I'll say to myself, you have plenty of good things laid up for many years. Take life easy; eat, drink, and be merry.'*

> *But God said to him, 'You fool! This very night your life will be demanded from you. Then who will get what you have prepared for yourself?'*

> *This is how it will be with anyone who stores up things for himself but is not rich toward God.*[2]

Our wealth can be taken from us literally in a heart-beat as Job discovered. If a person's wealth is not bringing honor and glory to God, He may ask why that person is still alive on the earth as He did to the rich fool. Wealth, like debt, must be used very circumspectly.

The Purpose for the Christian's Wealth

In the Sermon on the Mount, Jesus stated what Christian investments should achieve. There, Jesus said:

Do not store up for yourselves treasures on earth, where moth and rust destroy, and where thieves break in and steal. But store up for yourselves treasures in heaven, where moth and rust do not destroy, and where thieves do not break in and steal. For where your treasure is, there your heart will be also.[3]

A popular adage in the world today is: "He who dies with the most toys wins." Obviously, that belief contradicts the position that Jesus took in the Sermon on the Mount. Christians are to lay up treasures for eternity. All that will last in eternity will be the spiritual riches of souls which have accrued to our account. Everything else will be burned up. There will never be any U-Haul trailers behind a hearse.

Therefore, everything that Christians do should answer the following question—"Will this make any difference in light of eternity?" Any wealth that we accumulate should be designated to promote the kingdom of heaven; we are to lay up treasures in heaven and not on earth.

Some practical applications of Biblical principles of investing come from the "The Parable of the Talents" and "The Parable of the Pounds." While the main points of both parables are very similar, the details are quite different.

The Parable of the Talents

It is appropriate to define a parable as "an earthly story with a heavenly meaning." In Matthew 25:14-28, Jesus gave us the "Parable of the Talents" which is directly on point with modern investment principles. In the parable, Jesus described "a man traveling into a far country" (He was evidently a "mover and shaker" of his day) who gave three servants "talents," a monetary unit. He gave one servant five talents, another two, and another servant received one talent according to their abilities. Through "trading," each of the first two servants doubled their talents to ten and four respectively. Each of the two generated 100% return on the investment for the time allowed.

However, according to verse 18, the servant with one talent "went and digged in the earth, and hid his lord's money." In essence, he put his money into a hole in the ground. In his stewardship, he made absolutely nothing for his lord and had 0 % return on the investment.

The only good thing that can be said for him is that he did not lose it completely.

When the traveling man in the parable returned, each of the servants gave an accounting for the stewardship of the talents entrusted to them. Both of the first two proclaimed that they had doubled their lord's talents. Essentially, both were commended in the very similar ways. In verse 21, the servant who had increased his lord's talents from five to ten was given the following commendation:

> *His lord said unto him, well done, thou good and faithful servant: thou hast been faithful over a few things, I will make thee ruler over many things: enter thou into the joy of thy lord.*[4]

However, the servant who had hid the one talent was severely chastised and characterized as wicked and slothful. In verse 27, his lord said:

> *Well then, you should have put my money on deposit with the bankers so that when I returned I would have received it back with interest.*[5]

Verse 27 and the passage confirm the following:
1. Earning a return on an investment is not outside of the will of God.
2. "Whatever you do, work at it with all your heart, as working for the Lord, not for men."[6]
3. God expects us to invest.
4. Trading (time for assets or assets for assets) is an accepted form of commerce.

In effect, the parable provides for the potential for God's blessings through investments.

The Parable of the Ten Pounds (or) Minas

In Luke 19:11-27, the story-line of the parable of the ten pounds (KJV) or minas (NIV) is quite similar to the parable of the talents. However, in the parable of the ten pounds, a nobleman who was leaving to be subsequently crowned as a king gave ten servants 10 pounds each. After that, he said:

"Put this money to work...until I come back." [7]

If the nobleman in the parable is Jesus himself, then we are commanded to make investments until He returns as King.

In the parable of the ten talents, three of the ten servants provided their master with an accounting of their stewardship. The first servant made ten talents from his master's ten talents and received a very strong commendation from his master. The second servant's accounting disclosed that he had earned five pounds from the ten which had been entrusted to him and he also received a strong commendation.

However, the third servant's accounting revealed that he had taken the ten pounds and laid it away in a piece of cloth. Again, just as in the parable of the talents, he had a 0 % rate of return and his master castigated him accordingly. In verse 23, the servant's master stated:

> *Why then didn't you put my money on deposit, so that when I came back, I could have collected it with interest.* [8]

Once again, the master's criticism is virtually identical to what was provided in the parable of the talents. It also provides additional support for investing until the Lord returns.

Conclusions Concerning the Parable of the Talents and the Parable of the Pounds

Anytime anything is included in the Bible it is important. Moreover, when something is included in Scripture twice, *it is very important* and so it is with the two parables. It is a very strong endorsement of Christian investments and signifies its importance as a ministry. However, there are some forceful cautions against investments as well.

When Are Investments Wrong?

Whenever a person begins to trust investments as an idol, it is wrong. *For the love of money is a root of all kinds of evil. Some people, eager for money, have wandered from the faith and pierced themselves with many griefs.* [9] [Emphasis added.]

If investments cross over from being a Christian benefit to something that is worshiped in place of the Lord, then investments have become a god and cannot please God.

Examples of Biblical Wealth

Abraham

When it comes to the patriarchs, Abraham was God's "Main Man." As Abraham burst on the scene in the 12th Chapter of Genesis, this is the description found in the Amplified Bible:

> [1]*Now [in Haran] the Lord said to Abram. Go for yourself [for your own advantage] away from your country, from your relatives and your father's house, to the land that I will show you. [Heb. 11:8-10]*

> [2]*And I will make of you a great nation, and I will bless you [with abundant increase of favors] and make your name famous and distinguished, and you will be a blessing [dispensing good to others].*

> [3]*And I will bless those who bless you [who confer prosperity or happiness upon you] and curse him who curses or uses insolent language toward you; in you will all of the families and kindred of the earth be blessed [and by you they will bless themselves].*[10]

Of course, God had divinely ordained Abram (name later changed to Abraham) to be the father of the nation of Israel. God achieved this by Abraham fathering Isaac and Isaac, in turn, fathering Jacob (name later changed to Israel). Thereafter, Israel had twelve sons who became known as the twelve tribes of Israel and, subsequently, the nation of Israel. From the nation of Israel, God also provided the earthly father and mother of the "Messiah of the World"—Jesus Christ. Abraham, in fact, became one of the most important people on earth. What was Abraham's economic status?

The first description of Abraham's wealth and investments is found in Genesis 13:2: *"Now Abram was <u>extremely rich</u> in livestock and in silver and in gold."* (AMP) [emphasis added] In the second description, Abraham's wealth is greatly expanded:

The Lord has blessed my master and he has become very wealthy.
The LORD HAS GIVEN HIM SHEEP AND CATTLE,
SILVER AND GOLD, MALE AND FEMALE SERVANTS,
AND CAMELS AND DONKEYS.[11]

Abraham was used mightily by God and, in his day, had enormous wealth and investments. In turn, Abraham acknowledged God's provision of blessings and dedicated everything to bring honor and glory to God. Therefore, we can conclude that Abraham's great wealth was in line with God's will and was necessary for Abraham to achieve the goals that God had ordained for him. We, too, can use whatever wealth that God has given us to achieve His purposes.

Job

In his day, Job was a "Top Dog." In the first two chapters, the Bible describes Job in this way:

> *He possessed 7,000 sheep, 3,000 camels, 500 yoke of oxen, 500 female donkeys, and a very great body of servants, so that this man was the greatest of all of the men of the East.*[12] [Emphasis added.]

In the first of two tests, God allowed Satan to destroy all of the above assets, except for the messengers, in four back-to-back calamities. In addition, God allowed Satan to kill his seven sons and three daughters in the last calamity.

In the second test which followed on the heels of the first one, God allowed Satan to strike Job with painful boils from the "soles of his feet to the top of his head."[13] All of that was allowed even though Job was blameless and upright, feared God, and shunned evil.[14]

Essentially, for the next 35 chapters of Job, Job's "friends" [Eliphaz, Bildad and Zophar] and Job debated "the suffering of the righteous" and other related issues. In Chapters 38-41, the Almighty answered Job's questions with His own unanswerable questions. At the end,

> *Then Job replied to the Lord: "I know that you can do all things; no plan of yours can be thwarted.*[15]

In effect, Job acknowledged that God is omnipotent and that his questions to God were inappropriate. In a strange twist, God chastised Job's "friends" and then doubled Job's wealth over what it had been before his calamities.

> *The Lord blessed the latter part of Job's life more than the first. He had fourteen thousand sheep, six thousand camels, a thousand yoke of oxen and a thousand donkeys.*[16]

Also, God gave him another family and *"Nowhere in all of the land were found women as beautiful as Job's daughters…"*[17]

What are the conclusions that we can glean concerning Job's wealth? First, Job worshipped God and the Almighty blessed Job. We can expect the blessings of God only when we have surrendered everything that we have to Him. God subsequently allowed all of Job's wealth to be taken from him even though Job continued to praise and worship God. In His infinite wisdom, God knew what was best for Job. The same is true for each of us. When we are in a right relationship with God, all things are working together *for good* in accordance with Romans 8:28.

After his time of testing, God doubled Job's wealth. Can we expect comparable treatment? There are no assurances of that sort. Earlier, during the debates with his "friends," Job proclaimed: *"Though he slay me, yet will I trust in him…"*[18] and *"I know that my Redeemer lives, and that in the end he will stand upon the earth."*[19] He acknowledged that, regardless of what happened, God was going to reward him in life or in death.

Similarly, in the New Testament, Paul asserted: *"For to me to live is Christ and to die is gain."*[20] We need to do the same and use everything that we have for the glory of God and the proclamation of the gospel.

Never Envy Wealthy People—The Warning in Psalm 73

Psalm 73 is a very sober warning to wealthy people who do not know the love of God through Christ Jesus. Many arrogant rich individuals do not realize the wretched conditions that will make up their eternity if they reject the free gift of grace and mercy available through Jesus Christ.

In the REB, the writer of Psalm 73, Asaph, starts off the first verse with a very positive thought:

> *¹Assuredly God is good to the upright, to those who are pure in heart!*

After that, he describes his frustration with the wealthy is the following way in the first fourteen verses:

> *²My feet had almost slipped, my foothold had all but given way, ³because boasters roused my envy. ⁴No painful suffering for them! They are sleek and sound in body; ⁵they are not in trouble like ordinary mortals, nor are they afflicted like other folk.*

Then, Asaph continues his "pity party" through verse eleven. In verse 12, he concludes:

> *¹²Such are the wicked; unshakeably secure, they pile up wealth. ¹³Indeed it was all for nothing I kept my heart pure and washed my hands free from guilt.*

Not only were the wicked experiencing significant prosperity, but he was behaving righteously with little benefit to show for it.

However, in the next fourteen verses of Psalm 73, the tables are turned and the last become first.

In the NIV translation, we see the following:

> *¹⁶When I tried to understand all this, it was oppressive to me ¹⁷till I entered the sanctuary of God; then I understood their final destiny. ¹⁸Surely you place them on slippery ground; you cast them down to ruin. ¹⁹How suddenly they are destroyed, completely swept away by terrors.*

The KJV renders the last sentence in verse 19 as: "…they are utterly consumed by terrors." What a graphic description of their horrors! They have no cure for their ceaseless suffering.

In the New International Version of the Bible, Asaph finishes his discourse in the following way:

> *²⁰As a dream when one awakes, so when you arise, O Lord, you will despise them as fantasies. ²¹When my heart was grieved and*

my spirit embittered, ²²I was a senseless and ignorant; I was a brute beast before you. ²³Yet I am always with you; you hold me by my right hand. ²⁴You guide me with your counsel, and afterward you will take me into glory. ²⁵Whom have I in heaven but you? And earth has nothing I desire besides you.

We can summarize Psalm 73 in the following way: In the first fourteen verses, Asaph envies the wealthy and does not envision their everlasting fate. But, after entering the sanctuary of God, he foresees the horrible plight that they face in the eternal future. After that, he concludes in NIV verse 28:

²⁸But as for me, it is good to be near God. I have made the Sovereign God my refuge. I will tell of all of your deeds.

In effect, Asaph states the obvious: It is better to be content with God and have little wealth than to have great wealth and be headed for the "smoking section" of eternity.

Chapter Summary

Wealth is a two-edged sword. Wealth and investments can be used to achieve beneficial Christian objectives or for evil. The choice is ours.

Joseph of Arimathea was concurrently both a man of wealth and a disciple of Christ. Therefore, the two characteristics together are not mutually exclusive and are not necessarily vile.

According to both the parable of the talents and the parable of the pounds, investing is not inherently evil. In both of the parables, the slothful servant was chastised for not putting the entrusted money in the hands of a banker so that it would have at least drawn some interest. From both of those parables, we can see that investing may be in accordance with God's will when it is done properly.

However, there are some strong warnings concerning wealth and investments. When those two activities become an idol, then investments have crossed over into the wicked realm and cannot please God. After the discussion with the rich young ruler, Jesus said that it would be harder for a camel to go through the eye of a needle than for a rich man to enter heaven. The forceful point to be made is that we should be very careful with our wealth and use it for the glory of God.

Likewise, the parable of the rich farmer, who had no more room in his barns for his agricultural production and decided to tear them down and build bigger ones to store his produce, demonstrates the folly of misplaced priority on wealth. In the parable, God took his life and he enjoyed none of the wealth that he had accumulated.

In summary, wealth and investments dedicated to the furtherance of God's kingdom will be blessed. However, wealth and investments that are forms of idolatry cannot please God.

In the epistle of James, we are told:

> *When you ask, you do not receive, because you ask with wrong motives, that you may spend what you get on your pleasures.*[21]

We need to guard against wrong motives with our investments.

Chapter 9

INVESTMENTS IN REAL ESTATE USING GOD'S ABUNDANT ACRES FOR ABIDING ADVANTAGE

The Lord had said to Abram, "Leave your country, your people and your father's household and go to the land I will show you." **Genesis 12:1 (NIV)**

"Underneath all is the land." That statement demonstrates that all investments rely on land directly or indirectly. Land provides agricultural crops of all descriptions. It also yields natural resources such as petroleum, gold, and gravel. Moreover, economists may view production in terms of land, labor, and capital. In this chapter, we will review investments in real estate—"God's Abundant Acres for Abiding Advantage." In the last chapter, we saw that investments should provide treasures in heaven and not on earth. This is certainly true for real estate investments.

Land is one of the central themes in the Old Testament. The children of Israel were given land *"flowing with milk and honey."* [1] The opening books of the Old Testament focus on the trip to the land, possession of the land, and other actions surrounding the land. In Genesis, God told Abram (later Abraham):

> *Lift up now thine eyes, and look from the place where thou art northward, and southward, and eastward, and westward: For all the land which thou seest, to thee will I give it, and to thy seed forever.*[2]

Actually, Gentiles enjoy the same promise by virtue of the fact that they have been grafted into the Abrahamic tree.[3] However, as significant as that adopted heritage is, the New Testament de-emphasizes it in Paul's letter to the Galatians. There, he states:

> There is neither Jew nor Greek, there is neither bond nor free, there is neither male nor female: for ye are all one in Christ Jesus.[4]

Ultimately, God's promise to Abraham will be completely fulfilled. Until that time, what should our relationship to the land be? The question that Abner asked David, *"Whose is the land?"*[5], is an appropriate question for today. The answer is clearly given in the Psalm of Asaph, where God said:

> [9]*I have no need of a bull from your stall or of goats from your pens,* [10]*for every animal of the forest is mine, and the cattle on a thousand hills.* [11]*I know every bird in the mountains, and the creatures of the field are mine.* [12]*If I were hungry I would not tell you, for the world is mine and all that is in it.*[6]

Without question, all land everywhere belongs to God. At this time, it is "on loan" to us. In the early church, they handled real estate in the following manner:

> Neither was there any among them that lacked: for as many as were possessors of lands or houses sold them, and brought the prices of the things that were sold, and laid them at the apostles' feet...[7]

Today, it is not necessary to sell our real estate. However, it is necessary to utilize the revenues and gains to support God's work in a manner similar to the early church.

Ideal Real Estate

There are certain qualities which make real estate "ideal" for its intended purpose. It is incumbent on the real estate investor to pray and search for that "ideal" and obtain real estate which most closely measures up to that predetermined standard. When the descendants of Simeon were searching for pasture for their flocks:

They found rich, good pasture, and the land was spacious, peaceful and quiet.[8]

The adjectives: "rich, good, spacious, peaceful, and quiet" confirmed that the land met the requirements they wanted.

Likewise, if you are considering a real estate investment, it is a good idea to develop a set of standards so that you know exactly when real estate meets your specific requirements. In that way, you can remove some of the emotional considerations that may cloud your judgment.

Rental Real Estate

As a practical example, contemplated a rental real estate purchases generally require seven initial qualities:

1. "location, location, and location" (more on this later),
2. quality construction,
3. negative taxable income (because of the tax laws, this will not be appropriate for some taxpayers),
4. positive cash-flow for loan amortization and other expenses,
5. $50,000 in cost or less per unit (this is very difficult to find now),
6. appreciation potential, and
7. rental revenue = 1% of the fair market value of the property per month.

Maintaining positive cash-flow provides financing for the purchase of real estate essentially from the profits from the property without investing any additional out-of-pocket money. Moreover, the maximum investment of $50,000 per unit allows the rent to be a reasonable price and reduces vacancies. Appreciation potential keeps the investment sum at a minimum amount. Also, the 1% rule is another indicator of value. If the property will not generate 1% in rental revenue, it may be overpriced.

After the purchase, prospective tenants should complete a rental application where credit is examined and other references are reviewed. Once the application review is completed, then there should a written contract which requires a security deposit and payment up to the 1st of the next month for rent in advance. This process does not completely eliminate potential tenant difficulties, but it does reduce the probability for problems.

The Wrong Kind of Real Estate

In Genesis 11, the Bible describes the wrong kind of real estate in the following episode:

> *[1] Now the whole world had one language and a common speech. [2] As men moved eastward, they found a plain in Shinar and settled there. [3] They said to each other, "Come let's make bricks and bake them thoroughly." They used bricks instead of stone, and tar for mortar. [4] Then they said, "Come, let us build ourselves a city, with a tower that reaches to the heavens, so that we may make a name for ourselves and not be scattered over the face of the whole earth."* [9]

However, in verse 5 and following, the Lord God came down and reviewed the situation. God's conclusion was that they were engaged in prideful rebellion and idolatry. In verse 8, Scripture declares:

> *[8] So the Lord scattered them from there over all the earth, and they stopped building the city. [9] That is why it is called Babel—because there the Lord confused the language of the whole world. From there the Lord scattered them over the face of the whole earth.* [10]

What can we learn from this event concerning real estate? First, any real estate investment which does not bring honor and glory to God is destined to fail ultimately. If the purpose for the real estate is not an honorable one, God's blessings may be withheld. Second, if there is pride involved—"so that we can make a name for ourselves"—then Matthew 23:12 may come into play:

> *For whoever exalts himself will be humbled, and whoever humbles himself will be exalted.* [11]

It is interesting to compare the philosophy of the men of Babel where they wanted to "make a name for themselves" with Psalm 103:1-2. There, David proclaimed:

¹Bless the Lord, O my soul: and all that is within me bless his holy name. ²Bless the Lord, O my soul, and forget not all his benefits:[12]

In that passage, it is clear that King David wanted to lift up the name of the Lord instead of his own name.

The Wrong Way to Acquire Real Estate

Besides the wrong kind of real estate, it can be acquired in the wrong way. In I Kings, Naboth had a very nice vineyard that he had inherited from his fathers. The vineyard was so appealing that King Ahab coveted it and wanted to buy it. However, Naboth, in line with God's Word,[13] would not sell or trade it to Ahab. When he was rebuffed by Naboth, Ahab's "help meet," Jezebel, in her own "charming" way, said that she would give the vineyard to Ahab. In short order, she (1) arranged for a "contract" on Naboth, (2) had him stoned to death on false pretenses, and (3) did, in fact, give the vineyard to Ahab. But, in doing so, Jezebel's plot sealed her fate and pronounced disaster upon the family.[14] The sordid tale of Ahab and Jezebel is a classic example of how real estate should not be acquired.

In another Biblical illustration, Christ chastised the "teachers of the law" for the way they behaved and, specifically, for the way that they acquired some of their real property. In a very harsh discourse in Luke 20, He said:

⁴⁶Beware of the teachers of the law... ⁴⁷They devour widows' houses and for a show make lengthy prayers.[15]

Both of these examples reinforce Solomon's admonition:

No good comes of ill-gotten wealth.[16]

Quite clearly, an ill-gotten gain in real estate (or anything else) does not prosper. For long-term success, investments must be made in accordance with God's Will.

Application

A book of this nature cannot be an exhaustive compendium on the subject of real estate investments. But, there are certain basic principles and procedures to be utilized as well as pitfalls to be avoided. The remainder of this chapter will be devoted to coverage of those principles so that the serious investor may be motivated to seek the proper investment in accordance with predetermined investment objectives.

Liquidity

By its nature, real estate is generally not one of the most liquid of investments. Traded securities may be sold relatively quickly. In some cases, those securities can be sold in a few moments if the need for cash should arise. However, real estate may require a relatively long time to find a suitable buyer. Even after finding a buyer and signing a contract, the closing process can be a lengthy course of action. Many factors affect the length of time required to sell property such as interest rates, availability of mortgage money, intended use, return on investment, and others. It may be desirable to view proposed real estate acquisitions in light of future liquidity needs. More than one person has experienced substantial real estate appreciation but has been forced into a severe financial bind (even bankruptcy) because of cash-flow problems and lack of liquidity.

There may be ways of borrowing against the equity in the property. But, that option is not a certainty and must be viewed cautiously.

Return on Investment

In chapter one, we studied rate of return on the "perfect" investment. Real property has the potential to provide returns in the form of: (1) cash-flow, (2) appreciation, (3) income tax shelter, and (4) other psychological benefits.

Cash-Flow

Some investors wear t-shirts which proclaim: "Happiness is positive cash-flow." This is, indeed, an important position for investments. As it affects real estate investments, "positive cash-flow" is generally the excess of cash received from the realty over the cash required for the realty. In an "ideal" situation, revenue from the property will cover the debt service (loan principal reduction and interest expense) plus other operating expenses. Because it can be a self-liquidating debt (money received from the property covers the debt service), the only outlay of capital from the investor will be the down-payment. In effect, the investor uses O.P.M. (other people's money) to finance the property and will enjoy outright ownership with no debt when the loan is completely amortized and paid. In other words, the investor allows the users of the yield from the property to purchase the property for the investor with a minimum of personal capital required from the investor.

Also, even if the investor has to put some additional capital into the investment from time to time, the pro-rata amortization of the principal may allow the investor to recover that some of that outlay when the property is sold. For example, if $10,000 worth of real estate were acquired with a $1,000 down-payment and debt of $9,000, then the equity would be:

$$Assets \ = \ Debt \ + \ Equity$$

$$\$10,000 = \$9,000 + \$1,000$$

With a subsequent amortization of debt for $1,000 through debt repayment, then the equity becomes:

$$\$10,000 = \$8,000 + \$2,000$$

If we assume for illustrative purposes that the property is then sold for its original cost--$10,000, then the investor would receive $2,000 cash after the debt of $8,000 is paid off in the closing process. Each time that a loan payment is made and the loan principal owed is reduced, equity increases. In other words, some of the cash paid on the loan amortization, would ultimately be recovered.

Rate of Return on Investment

Rate of return may be calculated from a number of different viewpoints. Some of the more common methods are: (1), "equity," (2) "original cost," and (3) "fair market value." In the preceding section on cash-flow, if net income from the property were $1,000, then the rate of return on equity is:

$$net \ income/equity = \$1,000/\$1000 = 100\%.$$

However, if the return is calculated on (2) original cost, it becomes:

$$\text{net income/cost} = \$1,000/\$10,000 = 10\%$$

On the other hand, if the property has increased to $12,500, then the return (3) is:

$$\text{net income/fair market value} = \$1,000/\$12,500 = 8\%$$

Leverage and Calculation (1) and (2)

Calculation (1) demonstrates how "leverage" (using debt) increases return on investment. In calculation (1) the investor has invested 10% of the cost and the creditor has provided 90% of the cost with a mortgage as security for the loan. This strategy has the advantage of causing the return on investment to be ***ten times larger than it would have been*** if the investor had provided all of the capital as shown in calculation (2). This procedure is known as "leverage" where debt is used to lever the return on investor-provided capital.

At the same time, there is a ***danger*** associated with leverage. If the investment fails and does not provide the anticipated return on investment, the investor may lose the original investment, the investment property, and credibility for a Christian witness. The investor has made a promise to repay and, in effect, has broken his word thereby damaging his reputation. In the wisdom of Proverbs, Solomon declared:

A good name is more desirable than great riches; to be esteemed is better than silver or gold.[17]

A great deal of prayer, care, and caution are in order for leveraged real estate investments.

Analysis Based on Calculation (3)

Calculation (3) reveals an 8% return on investment and can be used to compare current returns with alternative options. For example, if the investment was earning 8% when comparable investments were yielding 10%, it could be an indication that: (a) revenues should be increased (i.e. raise rents), (b) expenses should be reduced, or (c) the property could be sold so that the current return can be achieved from the reinvestment of the proceeds from the sale.

Appreciation

After cash-flow returns from property, appreciation is a second form of return. Simply stated, appreciation is the increase in value of real property. In our inflationary economy, there is a high probability that property will go up in value if it is purchased at or below "fair market value" when acquired. On the other side of the coin, the less probable events of falling prices or static values may occur. Or, alternative investments may increase by a greater amount than real estate.

Depreciation

A third type of return comes in the form of income tax shelter through depreciation. Depreciation is the systematic allocation of the cost of an improvement to real estate throughout its estimated life and is authorized as a tax deduction by the Internal Revenue Code. To illustrate, if a $275,000 four-plex investment were made on owned land and the "tax life" of the rental unit had a 27.5 year life, then the calculation on a straight-line basis would be:

$$\$275,000/27.5 \text{ years} = \$10,000 \text{ per year depreciation}$$

The taxpayer benefits according to the marginal tax bracket. Generally, if a taxpayer were in a 28% tax bracket, then the $10,000 depreciation deduction would save $2,800 in taxes (28% of $10,000). However, in current tax law, these rules may become quite complicated with real estate "losses." If "modified adjusted gross income" goes above $100,000, then there are limitations on the deduction of real estate "losses" and the depreciation deduction may not provide the same amount of tax benefits. You, or your tax professional, should review your specific situation to determine the precise amount of benefits that will accrue to you for any proposed transactions. Also, bear in mind, that the tax "cost" or "basis" goes down with each depreciation deduction thereby making a subsequent sale provide a larger gain or a smaller loss.

The "Double Tax Shelter" for Certain Improved Real Estate

Because of inflation, some real estate provides a double tax shelter. In the $275,000 four-plex example above, the taxpayer would be able to take a depreciation expense of $10,000 even if the property was going up in value. For example, if the $275,000 four-plex increased 1% annually in value because of inflation, it would be worth $277,750 ($275,000 + 2,750). However, there would be no increase in taxable income or tax liability because of the increase in value until there is a sale or exchange of the property. In effect, there is a tax deduction of $10,000 for depreciation without a corresponding decline in value over the short-run and there would also be no tax to be paid on the $2,750 increase in value. This is known as the "double tax shelter" for certain improved real estate.

Psychological Benefits or Detriments

Another return accrues to people who enjoy the psychological benefits from owning property. Conversely, others perceive real property investments as a headache and a bothersome nuisance. Before investing in real estate, one should attempt to ascertain his or her leaning toward real property and take the appropriate action concerning this type of investment.

Types of Real Estate

There are various types of real estate for investment purposes. Each type should be considered when an investment decision is being contemplated.

Raw Land

The first option that we will cover is raw land. In this context, raw land is land without improvements and no known resources such as minerals, timber, or other salable commodities. In an urban setting, it is called a "vacant lot." Many people tend to view property investments retrospectively and say something like this: "If I had purchased that property in 1978, I would be worth a half million dollars today." What they are saying may be true. However, there is a very important concept to be considered here.

The concept to be considered here is the "Rule of 72." Simply stated, one can divide any rate of inflation into 72 and determine the length of time that it will take for the compounding effects of inflation to cut the purchasing power of the dollar in half. For example, a 12% rate of inflation will reduce the purchasing power of a dollar to fifty cents in 6 years (72 ÷ 12). Observing this phenomenon from the price of an asset, the rule means that property should double in price in 6 years with a 12% inflation rate.

From a slightly different vantage point, the compounding effects of saving $10,000 at a 10% rate of interest will produce $108,350 in only 25 years. If one could get a 16% interest rate, that same $10,000 would be worth $408,740 in 25 years and become $858,500 in 30 years! However, those returns are very unlikely today without incurring a huge amount of risk. Income taxes paid would also reduce those returns.

You may ask, "What does all that have to do with raw land?" The point is that while land goes up in price, so do alternative investments and one might discover that money drawing interest in a financial institution could produce even greater returns than those generated through appreciation in raw land prices.

The story of the tortoise and the hare demonstrates that consistent and steady progress toward a financial objective may be the best way to achieve that goal. Boiled down to the most elementary terms, raw land provides <u>no</u> positive cash flow and provides a return only through appreciation and/or tax deductions for property taxes which is a negative cash flow. Also, in order for the appreciation to be realized, the property must be sold or exchanged. In some instances, real estate is not the most liquid of assets and may take a considerable period of time to obtain any cash from the gain on the property.

Raw land may have the potential for better-than-average returns through development, rezoning, or some other influencing event, such as a new highway. Studying growth patterns, development trends, or other significant factors may provide knowledge for investment opportunities.

Land with Natural Resources

Land with natural resources can be analyzed by comparing the estimated returns from those assets with alternative investments having a similar risk factor. For example, land with timber may appreciate substantially because of increased demand and upward price pressures of inflation but that is not always the case.

Improved Real Estate Returns

Improved real estate has the potential to provide all types of returns that we have previously covered. However, there are additional return considerations that should be included in a proper evaluation. Additional returns should cover: (1) time spent, (2) risk incurred, and (3) capital required. Because management of property takes time, some return should compensate for the time required. For example, if a person's normal compensation is $15 per hour, then part of the return should compensate the investor for the time required when compared to alternative employments. After considering the time requirement, some investors believe that it is better economically to have an agent manage their property and oversee the agent. Next, a portion of the return should counter-balance the risk involved. One risk factor in this context is that the property will not remain rented. Another potential detriment is that the property could go down in value. Therefore, some of the returns should cover those contingencies and other risks. Last, the returns should provide for a return from the investment.

To illustrate, if an investment property cost $100,000 and generates $10,000 annual net income after taxes, then the return is 10% [$10,000 ÷ $100,000]. If 50 hours of management were required, then the time return is $750 [$15/hour x 50 hours]. If $1,000 per year is considered adequate return for the risk involved, then the return on capital is $8,250 or 8.25% return on capital. (See Exhibit 9-1)

EXHIBIT 9-1
Investment Returns

Time	$ 750
Risk	1,000
Capital	8,250
Total Returns	$10,000

The above analysis helps to place returns in the proper perspective and may be applied, not only to real estate, but any endeavor involving time, risk, and capital.

Additional Income Tax Benefits

In addition to depreciation and deferred recognition of gains until a sale or trade, there are other tax benefits associated with real estate. However, because (1) tax laws are some of the most complicated legal provisions known to man and (2) those laws are frequently changed by Congress or are interpreted in unique ways by courts, specific applications should be carefully researched by a competent tax adviser such as a C.P.A. who specializes in tax or a good tax attorney. The purpose of this section is to alert the investor to some of the benefits available through real property.

A. Deductions

Generally, all ordinary and necessary expenses associated with investment or business property are deductible. These include: interest, property taxes, insurance, repairs, operating expenses and many others. The benefits from those deductions are <u>limited</u> to the taxpayer's marginal tax rate and <u>never</u> provide a 100% cost recovery. In a 28% marginal tax bracket, a $100 repair expense will reduce taxes by only $28. The other $72 is a cost to be borne by the taxpayer.

B. Long-Term Capital Gains

In addition to beneficial deductions, gains on the sale of real property have the potential to provide long-term capital gain treatment where the property is held for "long terms." Long-term capital gains are currently subject to lower tax rates than other "ordinary" taxable income. For instance, if property which cost $10,000 were sold for $20,000, then the tax would be calculated in the following manner.

Sales Price	$20,000
Cost	$10,000
Gain	$10,000
Tax @ 20% rate	$ 2,000

If the taxpayer were otherwise in a 39.6% marginal tax bracket, then only $2,000 (20% x $10,000) would be paid in tax instead of $3,960

(39.6% of 10,000). In other words, the tax rate on other "ordinary" income would be almost double that of the capital gain. However, because of the "recapture" rules associated with real property and other complexities in the tax law, competent tax advice should be sought.

C. Installment Sales

An installment sale allows gains to be reported according to the cash received rather than having to recognize all of the gain at once. If property costing $60,000 were sold for $100,000, then the gain would be $40,000 [40% gross profit ratio]. But, if there was long-term contract and only $10,000 in cash were received in the year of sale, then 40% of $10,000 or $4,000 would be reported in taxable income. The other $36,000 in gains would be recognized by applying the 40% rate to the remaining $90,000 as it is collected. This method has the potential to defer gains over a longer period of time.

D. Other Tax Techniques

Many other tax techniques are available through real estate. The above factors have been included to alert investors to some of the common benefits available and to motivate them to consider those tax advantages which are uniquely available for their particular situation.

Rags to Riches

There are many "formulas" for making a "killing" in real estate. One approach which can be applied successfully is the "rags-to-riches" procedure. Patience is required in this technique because it may necessitate many evaluations before the "right" property is discovered. Basically, the procedure works in this manner: First, a suitable slightly "run-down" property (single family, multi-unit, or other) is located. This step generally requires perseverance in analyzing numerous properties before acquiring one. While exercising caution, it may be possible to let a property or two to slip by which subsequently turn out to be acceptable. This is not always bad and may give you greater confidence when the "right" property is discovered.

The prospective property should be superficially deteriorated but structurally sound (unless one has the capability to correct structural problems profitably). Ideally, a paint brush; lawn mower; hedge trimmer; hammer and nails; elbow grease; and minor "know-how" would be adequate to renovate the property. Regardless of the seeming triviality of the repair, a <u>list should be prepared</u> showing both the nature of the repair, and the estimated cost and/or time required for the repair. In some cases, a professional home inspector should be employed to evaluate the condition of the property and the cost to correct the defects.

If the repairs can be done in a profitable manner, then the next step is to make an offer on the property. If the cost of the property plus the needed repairs is less than the estimated fair market value of the property value after the repairs, then it may be an acceptable investment. The additional value comes from the labor expended and/or the negotiated skills exercised. For example, if one were to (1) pay $50,000 for a house, (2) spend $1000 repairing and renovating it, and (3) sell it for $55,000 after the repairs, then the labor (or "sweat-equity") and/or negotiating ability would be worth $4,000.

The offer is a critical point in the acquisition process. An offer to buy at a price slightly below the asking price will generally produce an acceptance or a subsequent counter-offer which can be accepted. However, some have bid below the asking price only to see the property slip away to someone who made a better offer. Therefore, to insure acquisition of the property, one should offer the asking price or appraised value whichever is less. On the other hand, if the property has been on the market for some time, the seller is desperate to sell, or other factors such as repossession are involved, then those circumstances may suggest that an offer significantly below the asking price might be accepted. In other words, each situation is unique and must be analyzed accordingly.

In addition, the offer should include the standard features of a real estate contract covering clear title to the land, termite inspection (if applicable), inspection of all working items and structural components of the property, division of closing costs, other appropriate items, and financing. Investors should shop for financing just like they shop for anything else and select the financing plan which is best for their unique situation.

Utilization

Once the property has been acquired and renovated, investors can opt to sell it (hopefully for a profit) or generate revenue through rents. If a rent increase can be justified because of the renovation, this, in turn, may increase the value of the property subsequently.

Physical Characteristics

Proximity to churches, schools, transportation, shopping, and work are important. Traffic noise, airport flight patterns, industrial pollution, and a host of other factors should be considered. Many real estate specialists believe the three most important characteristics of real estate, in rank order, are: "location, location, and location." This criterion can hardly be over-emphasized.

Summary

Throughout recorded history, real estate has been a special investment and continues to enjoy that favored status to the present time. There are significant returns and tax benefits associated with real estate investments. Patience, perseverance, and knowledge pay big dividends in the acquisition process. Profit potential through real estate renovation and/or development is limited only by the human imagination. There are many formulas for significant real estate investment returns including the "rags-to-riches" concept and other variations. "Underneath all is the land."

Chapter 10

INVESTMENTS IN SECURITIES: GOOD OR EVIL?

It is like a man going abroad, who called his servants and entrusted his capital to them; Then he left the country. **Matthew 25:14,15b (REB)**

Since: (1) the Great Depression of 1929 and the following economic dislocation of the 1930's, (2) Black Monday of October 19, 1987 where the Dow-Jones Industrial Average dropped a record 508 points, (3) the technology stock bubble bursting in the late 1990's, and (4) other "corrections" in the stock market, investments have been out of favor for some investors. It is quite easy to see where that view-point originated. Many saw large fortunes annihilated when the stock market collapsed. Some watched their retirement plans decimated because of fraud as in the case of Enron and others. Today, some still feel that history could repeat itself and securities should be avoided.

Therefore, every security investment should be evaluated very carefully. It is a necessary requirement to: "Investigate before you invest." That investigation should be very thorough and should provide potential investors with complete "peace of mind" *before* they make any investments. Time, energy, and expertise should be focused on potential risks and rewards of alternatives prior to committing to any venture. Beware! Rewards come from *future* events which are always unknown.

With that backdrop as a <u>*heavy warning*</u>, let us turn our attention to the background of securities. First, what are securities? Securities are nothing more than "paper representations" of the right side of the balance sheet equation:

Assets = Liabilities + Ownership Equity

Thus, securities come in two basic forms: (1) debt and (2) ownership equity. Investors who have invested in the debt of a corporation or other entity are considered creditors while those who invest in ownership equity are the owners of the corporation. Both have quite different relationships with the corporation. Creditor investors may own debentures, mortgage bonds, equipment trust instruments, "junk bonds," or a host of other debt instruments. The payment return that they receive for interest is usually required to meet the provisions of the indenture or other contract associated with the debt. Also, at the maturity of the debt instrument, the investor is entitled to receive the principal back on the loan.

There are two ways that an investor can benefit from securities investments—(1) interest earned or dividends received, or (2) capital appreciation. In addition, there are two ways that an investor can suffer loss from securities investments—(1) not receiving anticipated interest or dividends and (2) capital value decline. Once again, there is potential financial peril associated with securities investments. Therefore, investors should match their comfortable risk level with expected reward for that level of risk. The general rule is that for a greater risk there should be potential for greater reward. Conversely, a lower risk generally should provide lower rewards.

Basic Debt Operation

For example, in essence, an investment in a $1000 corporate bond which pays 6% per year payable semi-annually on January 1 and July 1 and matures in 2020 would function in the following way. The bondholder would receive $30 (half of $60 annual interest) on January 1 and $30 on July 1 until 2020. If the bondholder sells the bond between interest payment dates, the interest accrues and is paid to the bondholder when the bond is sold. In 2020, the $1000 principal should be repaid by the corporation. Failure of the corporation to meet those required payments could result in default and subsequently trigger legal action on behalf of the creditors. In the event of a corporate liquidation (or bankruptcy), the creditors should be paid before any of the owners are paid.

Basic Debt Risk

In practice, even though all creditors are paid before any equity holders are paid in the event of liquidation, ***there is always risk associated with debt instruments before they mature because of interest fluctuations and other market factors.*** For example, if a 5% AAA $1000.00 bond were purchased, then the investor would earn $50 annually. However, if market forces, including any Federal Reserve decisions, caused interest rates for comparable AAA bonds to go up to 6%, then the 5% bonds market value could be adjusted appropriately and very severely. The $50 (5%) bond could be discounted to a point where it now yields 6% in the market in the following way:

$$\$50/\$833 = 6\%$$

In other words, the $1000.00 bond could be discounted to $833.33 because of the increase in interest rates. In that case, a sale of the $1000.00 bond *before maturity* would provide a loss of $166.67. This is only one of several risks associated with debt.

Basic Equity Operation

For equity investors on the other hand, the owners of a corporation *initially* purchase common or preferred stock from the corporation. However, once the common or preferred stock is purchased initially, it can be sold from one investor to another and the corporation gets nothing directly from those transactions. Unlike the bond example above where the interest payment is generally mandatory, the stockholders may receive quarterly dividends which is a discretionary decision by the board of directors.

Common Stock vs. Preferred Stock

If a corporation has only one class of stock, that class will be common stock. The basic rights of common stockholders are: (1) the right to vote for the directors, (2) the right to receive dividends, ***if declared***, (3) the right to receive a pro-rata portion of the assets after all creditors and preferred stockholders have been paid in the event of a liquidation, and (4) the pre-emptive right, if it has not been voted out by the stockholders. The pre-emptive right is the ability to maintain a stockholder's percentage of ownership when new shares are issued. Other rights which are generally present are: the right to vote for the auditor, the right to vote on approved stockholder resolutions, and the right to transfer shares to other potential stockholders. However, in some small closely-held corporations, the right to transfer is restricted.

On the other hand, if a corporation issues a second class of stock, it will typically be preferred stock. The term "preferred stock" does **_not_** mean that it is superior or "more desirable" than other investments but that it receives some preference, where appropriate. Preferred stock may be preferred over common stock when dividends are declared, when asset distributions are made in the event of a liquidation, or, generally, both dividend declarations and liquidating asset distributions. Preferred stock is sometimes considered to be "in between" debt and equity because it has some characteristics of debt, such as dividend preference, but is still shown in the equity section of the balance sheet and considered an "ownership security."

Basic Equity Risk

At any time, dividends can be increased, stopped, or lowered based on the criteria which the directors use to make decisions at that moment. Also, dividends do not accrue and are paid to stockholders which are owners at the beginning of business on the "date of record." In addition, there is no "maturity date" for common or preferred stock and the only way that an investor can recover an investment is by selling the investment to another party at a price that is determined by market forces. The market price received may be higher or _lower_ than the original cost to the investor providing a gain or _loss_ on the investment. Obviously, there is always **_risk_** associated with any investment except the "perfect investment" described previously in chapter 1.

Where Are Securities Discussed in the Bible?

Our modern securities system was set up as a means to raise capital by men long after the Bible was written and, therefore, has nothing written directly regarding our current system. However, there are some concepts which are discussed in the Bible which have direct application to our modern securities system. For example, The Revised English Bible states:

> *It is like a man going abroad, who called his servants and entrusted his capital to them; ... Then he left the country.*[1]

Every time that an investor makes an investment in a security, his capital is entrusted to some individual, firm, or institution and virtually all business decisions concerning that investment are made by others. The directors have a responsibility to handle their stewardship prudently and wisely on behalf of the investor. Unfortunately, some directors and officers (including WorldCom, Enron, and others) have broken that trust and have plundered the capital of many unsuspecting investors.

Investments in securities are based on trust. However, recent frauds have confirmed that the trust which was anticipated has been misplaced and abused. Once again, insofar as it is possible, thorough investigations should be performed prior to making any investment.

Expecting God's Blessing for Security Investment

It seems obvious that securities which promote sin or other dishonest endeavors should be avoided by Christian investors. Firms which are engaged in production of tobacco products, alcoholic beverages, gambling, and other sinful practices cannot expect God's blessings over the long-term. Unfortunately, some companies which function on sound Christian principles and were started by successful Christian leadership are now amalgamated into corporations operated for questionable purposes. Furthermore, many mutual funds have very small fractions of their investments in morally challenged industries or companies. What should a righteous investor do in these cases?

That answer compares similarly to the "meat sacrificed to idols" example at the time of Paul and his letter to the Corinthian church. Paul stated:

> *Here's what you should do. You may eat any meat that is sold in the marketplace. Don't ask whether or not it was offered to idols,*

and then your conscience won't be bothered. For "the earth is the Lord's and everything in it."

If someone who isn't a Christian asks you home for dinner, go ahead; accept the invitation if you want to. Eat whatever is offered to you and don't ask any questions about it. Your conscience should not be bothered by this. But suppose someone warns you that this meat has been offered to an idol. Don't eat it, out of consideration for the conscience of the one who told you. It might not be a matter of conscience to you, but it is for the other person.

Now, why should my freedom be limited by what someone else thinks? If I can thank God for the food and enjoy it, why should I be condemned for eating it? Whatever you eat or drink or whatever you do, you must do all for the glory of God.[2]

While Paul's advice to the Corinthian church is not perfect concerning investment matters, perhaps there are some truths which apply. First, if any investment is primarily known for its questionable activities, regardless of what they are, then that investment should be avoided. On the other hand, if those undesirable practices are unknown to you at the time of the investment decision, then the investment may be acceptable. However, once the undesirable practices are known, you must make a moral choice about the continuation of the investment. Everything that is done on earth should bring honor and glory to God.

Diversification—"Don't Put All of Your Eggs in One Basket"

One of the best principles of securities investment (and other business ventures as well) is to diversify your investments. In other words, "Don't put all of your eggs in one basket." Then, if one investment fails, the expectation is that the other investments will compensate for the loss with gains and returns. For example, those Enron employees who had virtually all of their retirement investment in Enron stock, lost their nest egg completely when Enron went bankrupt. If they had diversified their retirement savings into other conservative investments besides Enron, they would still have suffered a loss but it would have been a small fraction of their retirement portfolio and they subsequently would have had a sizable retirement fund for their needs.

The Revised English Bible verse which supports the diversification principle is found in Ecclesiastes. It states:

> *Divide your merchandise among seven or perhaps eight ventures, since you do not know what disasters are in store for the world.*[3]

By comparative analysis, this section of the Bible must be very difficult to translate into modern idiomatic English because other translations of the Bible are quite different. The verse before the one above in the King James Version says:

> *Cast thy bread upon the waters: for thou shalt find it after many days.*[4]

Obviously, translators have struggled with the original meaning in this portion of the Bible because there are quite different passages in various translations. However, each translation could essentially state: "Don't put all of your eggs in one basket."

Managed Accounts—Application of the Diversification Principle

Many individual investors are financially unable to diversify properly. In those cases where investors have the inability to diversify adequately, managed investments may be very beneficial. By having multiple investors, hundreds or thousands, managed investments can pool their money and then diversify acceptably. The managed investment investor subsequently owns a pro-rata share of an adequately diversified pool of investments or index funds.

The decision to purchase managed investments is one which requires research on the part of the investor. When time is a precious commodity, a trusted professional may be able to provide value for service rendered. Total long-term costs and expected returns should be carefully compared to maximize benefits.

Also, managed investments provide an application of the following verse:

> *Plans fail for lack of counsel, but with many advisers they succeed.*[5]

Individual investment managers have superiors who are reviewing decisions and results. In that process, "two heads are better than one" and provide some checks and balances in the investment process.

Caution—Managed Investment May Also Provide Investment Losses

Even though managed investments have many benefits associated with them, they are *not immune from loss*. When the general market goes down, managed investments may also follow the path down. In some cases, managed investments may go down in an "up" market. In any case, mutual funds or other index funds are guaranteed to perform in one of three ways: go up, stay the same, or go down. Once again, there is risk in any investment.

A Comparison of Real Estate vs. Stock Investments

Real estate can be extremely illiquid in some cases whereas listed securities can be sold very quickly. There are "headaches" in real estate management including vandalism, never-ending maintenance, and collection challenges. Some pundits maintain that if you own five or more toilets, you have a job rather than an investment. Depreciation provides legal tax shelter for real estate which does not exist for stock. Also, leverage tends to be greatest in real estate. In summary, each individual must assess their personality, goals, and the risks and rewards of each investment and make choices. Fortunately, the two investments are not mutually exclusive and both are possible at the same time. It may also be that one will be superior over the other at different stages in a person's life. However, it may be that neither has any appeal and the investor may opt for government bonds or bank certificates of deposits. It is wonderful to live where we are free to make choices that we believe are best for us. Praise God!

Chapter Summary

Security investments provide a way for financial growth and prosperity. At the same time, there may be substantial risk present in those investments. There is no substitute for a thorough investigation of any proposed investment *prior* to that investment—"Investigate before you invest."

Diversification is a desirable investment principle for almost all investments and business ventures. "Don't put all of your eggs in one basket."

Last of all, there is **_RISK_** in every investment. An investor must recognize the risk involved and be certain to take that into account when evaluating the potential reward from any investment option.

Chapter 11

TAXES—RENDER TO CAESAR THOSE THINGS WHICH ARE CAESAR'S

...Render therefore unto Caesar the things which are Caesar's and unto God the things that are God's. **Matthew 22:21b**

And it came to pass in those days, that there went out a decree from Caesar Augustus that all the world should be taxed. **Luke 2:1**

In the absence of the "rapture," most would agree that there are two certainties in this life—death and taxes. While many people complain about taxes, Jesus stated imperatively in Matthew 22:21 that we are to render unto Caesar (the government of that day) the *things* which are Caesar's and unto God the things that are God's. Therefore, prompt and courteous payment of taxes is required for every Christian.

Actually, the only thing worse than paying taxes is not to having to pay any tax at all. Because of the alternative minimum tax and other provisions in the tax law, paying no tax generally means that a person has not worked or invested for a year. It could also be an indicator that a person may be very close to illegal tax evasion. Acting to benefit some wealthy taxpayers, recent tax frauds have threatened the viability of large international CPA firms and some prominent legal practices. Personally, this author is thankful to have to pay taxes because that allows me to enjoy the benefits and opportunities of the greatest country on earth.

Tax Planning

Now, having said that, it is also crystal clear that taxpayers do not want to pay any more tax than they legally have to pay. Astute students of taxation spend a great deal of time and effort to reduce their long-term tax liability. In addition, the courts have long upheld the right of citizens to minimize their tax obligation within the law. When tax planning is boiled down to the lowest level, there are three major principles of U. S. income tax planning:

1. Minimize revenue recognition.
2. Maximize deductions.
3. Take advantage of all other beneficial tax provisions.

Minimize Revenue Recognition

There are some remaining ways to minimize revenue recognition. For example, investors can reduce their tax liability by investing in qualifying "municipal bonds" or some type of mutual fund with qualifying "municipal bonds." Qualifying "municipal bonds" are usually the general bond obligations of states or their political subdivisions including counties, parishes (Louisiana only), cities, and towns. When qualifying "municipal bonds" are purchased, then generally the interest earned is exempt from federal income tax. Examples of qualifying "municipal bonds" would be general obligation bonds of the state of Texas, Dallas County, or the City of Dallas. In some cases, bonds issued by those entities could be considered non-qualifying bonds and the interest would be subject to federal income tax. Obviously, it is absolutely essential to confirm the tax-exempt interest status of any contemplated "municipal bond" acquisition ***before*** the purchase is made.

There are also other ways by which taxable revenues can be reduced. However, seeking technical advice from a competent and trusted tax adviser is generally a good first step for lowering taxable revenues.

Plans go wrong for lack of advice; many counselors bring success.[1]

By reducing taxable revenues, taxable income will be simultaneously reduced. That, in turn, will decrease the amount of tax to be paid.

Maximize Tax Deductions

To reduce taxable income, tax deductions should be maximized. There are three primary Internal Revenue Code Sections (IRC) which allow deductions for specified expenses or defined losses:

IRC Section 162 generally allows all "ordinary and necessary" business expenses which includes expenses of a trade, business, or profession on Form 1040 Schedule C or expenses of farming on 1040 Schedule F. However, as is virtually always the case, there are exceptions to those general rules and advice from a tax professional may be desirable and valuable.

Expenses for investment and tax advice are typically deductible based on IRC Section 212. Specifically, expenses "for the production of income" (investment) and for the "management, maintenance, or conservation" of income producing properties (most rental property expenses) are deductible, but may be limited. Also, expenses incurred for the determination, collection, or refund of any tax may be deductible.

Deductions for losses are authorized by IRC Section 165. Losses associated with a trade, business, or profession are generally deductible. Also, losses incurred in investments are characteristically deductible. However, losses on the biggest investment that many people have, their personal residence, are not authorized by IRC Section 165. The last part of IRC Section 165 prescribes the types of casualty losses (natural calamities and theft) which are deductible. Most net business casualties are fully deductible. But, personal casualty losses have so many technicalities that they will typically be non-deductible. If it is a close call as far as deductibility is concerned, it would probably be desirable to calculate the deduction to determine the amount to ascertain whether it is a beneficial deduction or whether the standard deduction would be desirable.

In addition, itemized deductions or the "standard deduction" reduce taxable income. Taxpayers are allowed to take the *greater* of the "standard deduction" or itemized deductions. The "standard deduction" is an amount which Congress designates as a deduction without any additional documentation on the part of the taxpayer. On the other hand, itemized deductions include specified medical expenses, certain taxes, qualified charitable contributions, mortgage interest on up to two personal residences, and "other itemized deductions." However, all of those categories have technical points that must be observed for the deduction to be appropriate.

By maximizing deductions, tax liabilities may be dramatically reduced. To achieve tax reduction through maximizing deductions, taxpayers must become knowledgeable concerning those deductions which are legally deductible. Or, alternatively, they must consult a qualified tax professional who can assist them in that determination.

Take Advantage of All Other Tax Provisions

There currently are many other strategies which can reduce tax obligations. Special tax rates for long-term capital gains, income averaging for farmers, lower tax rates on dividends, special depletion allowances for individual oil and gas royalties are only a few of the legal opportunities that are available for tax reduction. However, all special provisions can be changed or eliminated quickly by Congress. Ignorance of the law may be very costly in tax compliance.

A Very Strange Tax Payment

Once, in Capernaum, Peter was asked if Jesus was going to pay the Temple tax. Peter affirmed that Jesus would pay the tax and subsequently went into the house to talk to Jesus about it. Moreover, Jesus knew what he was going to ask even before he arrived. Jesus started the conversation by implying that the Temple tax was probably not applicable to him or Peter. Then Jesus said:

> However, we don't want to offend them, so go down to the lake and throw in a line. Open the mouth of the first fish you catch, and you will find a coin. Take the coin and pay the tax for both of us.[2]

Please note that the tax was not paid to a governmental unit but to the collectors of the Temple tax.

What is the significance of the anecdote for us today? One interpretation could be that even when we do not agree with the system of taxation, we are still obligated to pay legitimate taxes. Protests over methods and purposes for taxes may be counterproductive for the Christian. From my perspective, I am still waiting for the fish which has my tax obligation in its mouth. Please let me know if you have caught a fish with your tax liability contained inside its mouth.

Chapter Summary

We are to render unto Caesar (the government of our day) those things that are Caesar's and unto God those things which are God's. In other words, we are to pay our taxes with a Christian attitude. However, interpretations by the U. S. Supreme and the Bible declare that we do not have any more liability than the law requires. There are three grand principles of income tax planning: (1) "minimize revenue" through exclusion or deferral, (2) "maximize deductions" by taking advantage of all legal reductions, and (3) taking advantage of all other tax saving provisions in the law.

Chapter 12

RETIREMENT—THE GOLDEN YEARS: REDUNDANT OR REJOICING?

Moses was a hundred and twenty years old when he died,
yet his eyes were not weak, nor his strength gone. **Deuteronomy 34:7 (NIV)**

As for the days of our life, they contain seventy years, or if due to strength,
eighty years, yet their pride is but labor and sorrow; For soon it is gone
and we fly away. **Psalm 90:10 (NASB)**

…but at age fifty, they must retire from their regular service and work no longer.
Numbers 8:25(NIV)

For many, retirement is perceived as the closest echelon near heaven that can be experienced on this earth. They no longer have to work and can do those things that they have been unable to do while they were employed—travel, visit, spend more time in recreation, or serve the Lord in a more effective manner with the extra time that becomes available. Should a Christian retire? If so, what age is the right age for retirement?

The Bible does not emphasize retirement as heavily as it does many topics. However, there are some guidelines that are presented to assist in retirement decisions. First, there are some general principles concerning our Christian service during our lifetime whether we are employed or retired.

Five Overriding Christian Principles for Life

I. As Jesus was being questioned by the "expert on the law" dealing with life forever, Jesus asked him about his understanding of the Scriptures concerning that issue. The expert stated that you should:

"Love the Lord your God with all your heart, all your soul, all your strength, and all your mind." Also, "Love your neighbor as you love yourself." [1]

This is true for both active and retirement years.

II. In Ecclesiastes, King Solomon reviewed a number of topics "under the sun" (on earth) and came to this general conclusion concerning life:

Fear God and keep His commandments. [2]

Once again, this is appropriate regardless of a person's age or station in life.

III. In the minor prophet book of Micah, we find a gold nugget of Christian behavior in the following:

He has shown you, O man, what is good; and what does the Lord require of you but to do justly, to love mercy, and to walk humbly with your God? [3]

That is a short sentence but it is loaded with profound truth for youth and adults.

IV. In the book of Deuteronomy, Moses provides the following very sagacious wisdom:

And now, O Israel, what does the Lord your God ask of you but to fear the Lord your God, to walk in all his ways, to love him, to serve the Lord with all your heart and with all your soul, and to observe the Lord's commands and decrees that I am giving you today for your own good? [4]

Moses's statement could be considered a summary admonition for the other three principles for life above.

V. In the 11th chapter of Deuteronomy, Moses specifies the necessary requirement for God's blessings each day of our lives. We choose from the two options that are included in the following section:

> *Behold, I set before you a blessing and a curse: the blessing if you obey the commandments of the Lord your God which I command you today; and the curse if you do not obey the commandments of the Lord your God…*[5]

The choice is ours: to obey or not to obey.

Whether we are gainfully employed or enjoying the benefits of retirement, we should apply each of the five overriding Christian principles on a daily basis. The fifth principle demonstrates how to receive God's blessings continuously during our life.

Christian Retirement Decisions

Should a Christian retire? The Old Testament provides some ground rules in the 8th chapter of Numbers. In that section, there are some specific ages given which may serve as guidelines for today but may not be applied literally in all cases. Let's review that section of God's Word for direction on the matter of retirement.

In the 8th chapter of Numbers, Moses set the Levites apart to do the work at the Tent of Meeting on behalf of Israelites and to make atonement for them.[6] After that:

> *The Lord said to Moses, "This applies to the Levites: Men twenty-five years old or more shall come take part in the work at the Tent of Meeting, but at the age of fifty, **they must retire** from their regular service and work no longer. They may assist their brothers in performing their duties at the Tent of Meeting, but they themselves must not do the work. This, then, is how you are to assign the responsibilities of the Levites."*[7] (emphasis added)

In that working environment, it is very clear that God commanded that men twenty-five or more were to perform the work at the Tent of

Meeting until they reached age fifty. At that point, they were to retire with the proviso that they could assist with the work but not actually do the work.

What are the principles that apply in this specific case which can be applied generally in other work environments? There are three general principles present in this passage.

1. First, there is an age at which a person should start employment. In this case, it was twenty-five.
2. Second, there is an age at which a person should retire. Here, it is fifty.
3. Last, there is meaningful service after retirement. They could assist in the work. However, they were not required to actually do the work.

These general principles can be applied in any working arena. But, they probably should not be taken literally for all venues. This paragraph confirms the position that work retirement is appropriate for Christians who desire to do so.

To review, there is a starting point for employment. After a person has the necessary training and/or education and has both the physical and mental stamina to do the work, they should begin work. In this section, God was satisfied that they were sufficiently trained at twenty-five to perform the service. It could certainly be another age in other endeavors.

Also, retirement was *required* at age fifty. God did not disclose His reasons for age fifty but there is no doubt about that age. The U.S. military has a current mandatory retirement age of 62 for officers. However, many qualify for retirement before age 62 and may retire at a younger age. Different organizations and institutions have other retirement requirements. None of these requirements conflict with the concepts in this section of God's Word.

Perhaps the burning question that some have is: May I continue meaningful service after I retire? Nothing is stated in the passage about alternative employments after retirement except for assistance with the work that they had been doing. Many today retire only to discover that they would be happier back in the work force. Some start new careers. Others go to work for another employer in the same general type of employment or go back to their former employer. Let's examine the retirement of Moses and King David for additional insights into God's plan for retirement.

Moses's "Retirement"

The life of Moses can be divided into three forty-year time frames. In the first forty years, Moses, a Jew, was considered to be the son of the Egyptian Pharaoh because of divine influence at his birth.[8] During that time frame, Moses received the best formal training and education that a member of the Egyptian royal family could receive in that day and age.

At age 40, Moses saw an Egyptian beating a Hebrew, one of his own people. He became incensed and slew the Egyptian on the spot when he *thought* that no one was looking.[9] However, the Pharaoh learned about Moses's homicide and intended to kill him in return. It was at that point that Moses fled from the Pharaoh and ended up on the "backside of the desert" tending his father-in-law's sheep. Moses fell from one of the highest positions in society to one of the lowest because of his sin. In due time, Moses received his "Bachelor of Science" in "Desertology" to prepare him for his next assignment.

As an octogenarian, *yes*, at age 80; Moses was commissioned by God from a burning bush to go back to Egypt and lead the children of Israel out of Egypt and into Canaan, the "promised land flowing with milk and honey."[10] With forty years of royal formal education and another forty years of "on-the-job" training in the desert, Moses had the exact training and experience that God desired for his final job of service—to lead the children of Israel into the "promised land." From age 80 to age 120, Moses led the Hebrew children through many trying times up to the border of Canaan and actually saw the "promised land." But, he did not cross over into that land.[11]

When did Moses retire? We may retire from a secular working position but Christians never retire from Christian service and witness for the Lord until our earthly departure. Moses proved that.

King David's Retirement

David, son of Jesse, was not born into a royal family but was anointed to be king of Israel by God. In fact, he was first introduced as a shepherd boy tending his father's sheep. David and Moses shared that common ground—both were shepherds at some time in their lives. God referred to David as: "a man after my own heart."[12] King David's life was very thrilling and filled to overflowing with challenging times, successful times, and warts, also known as sins.

How could David be a man after God's own heart when he: (1) committed adultery with Bathsheba, (2) had Bathsheba's husband, Uriah, slain in battle, and (3) caused some more troops to be killed when Uriah was "set up" to die? It was obviously an attempt to cover up his sin with Bathsheba.[13] However, God is omniscient and knew all about David's intentions and actions when the thought of sin was first conceived in his mind. The answer to that question is found in Psalm 51 where David poured out his heart before God and requested forgiveness. Of course, God forgave him and removed his sin as far as the east is from the west. However, the consequences of David's sin continued.

When did David retire? To some degree, David retired when he could not keep warm even when they put covers over him.[14] However, David continued to be king until his death and his son, Solomon, became king. In effect, David retired when God retired him just as Moses retired before him. Once again, Christian servants retire when God ordains it. As long as God desires Christian service from an individual, they will be blessed by continuing the ministry that God gives them.

Retirement Resources

How much is needed for an adequate retirement? Ideally, individuals should have financial resources that will provide for the rest of their lives. In practice, we do not know how long we are going to live or the impact that other factors, such as inflation, will have on our standard of living. As was covered in chapter 3, we need to plan ahead much like the builder of a house or a commander going to battle. Also, we have the promise from God that He will meet all of our needs according to his riches in glory by Christ Jesus.[15] "Do not be anxious for anything, but in everything, by prayer and petition; with thanksgiving, present your requests to God."[16] We can generally adapt our retirement to the resources that God has provided.

Chapter Summary

There is no prohibition against a person retiring from a secular position. The time of retirement is an individual decision for the person involved and should be considered based on health conditions, physical and mental energy available, and retirement resources, both now and projected into the future. Some have discovered to their dismay that what was once a good retirement income has been dissipated over time by inflation or other unexpected factors. However, God will always provide for our needs regardless of the situation according to Philippians 4:19.

Chapter 13

STEWARDSHIP—GIVING OUR TIME AND RESOURCES: GOD LOVES A CHEERFUL GIVER

"…Bring all the tithes into the storehouse so there will be enough food in my Temple. If you do," says the Lord Almighty, "I will open the windows of heaven for you. I will pour out a blessing so great you won't have enough room to take it in! Try it! Let me prove it to you!…" **Malachi 3:10 (NLT***)*

This Old Testament verse is often used by pastors in an attempt to get church members to tithe (10%) to the church. Is that verse an appropriate guideline? Absolutely! Is it etched in granite? Hardly. That verse is a legal concept and most pastors will emphasize heavily that we are under grace rather than the law. However, if, under grace, you are looking for a "loophole" that will allow you to contribute less than the tithe, forget it.

The Widow's Mite

What was the example for giving that Jesus used in the New Testament? The teaching illustration that Jesus presented was the widow's "mite" (KJV). That passage unfolds in the following way:

Jesus sat down opposite the place where the offerings were put and watched the crowd putting their money into the temple treasury. Many rich people threw in large amounts. But a poor widow came and put in two very small copper coins worth only a fraction of a penny. Calling his disciples to him, Jesus said, "I tell you the truth, this poor widow has put more into the treasury than all of the others. They gave out of their wealth; but she, out of her poverty, put in everything—all she had to live on." [1]

How did Jesus know how much was given by each contributor? Jesus is God and is omniscient. He knows every mental image we have and has the hairs on our head numbered. Moreover, He knows the thoughts and intents of our heart.[2] What are the principles that Jesus emphasized in the story of the widow's mite? The fact that the incident is included in both Mark and Luke attests to its importance. First, Jesus is impressed with the amount of the sacrifice rather than the amount of the gift. The poor widow "put more into the treasury than all the others" even though it may have been the smallest donation. She made the greatest sacrifice of all of the givers because she gave everything that she had to live on.

Second, ten percent is a starting point but not the upper boundary. If we are ever in doubt about what we should contribute to God's work, we should give the higher amount rather than the lower. God does not "need" anything that we have. He has the cattle on a thousand hills and the entire world is His.[3] He wants us to give on earth so that we can lay up treasures in heaven.[4] By giving away, we ultimately have more. This is one of a number of paradoxes that we have in Scripture.

Was the widow singled out for a special blessing from God? The passage is silent on that issue and we are told nothing more about the widow. God is not like a vending machine where we put our money in and out comes our merchandise. No, many of our rewards will not be received on earth but will be distributed in heaven. We need to give without expecting direct benefit as a result of the gift. One thing is certain. The poor widow will be rewarded in heaven.

Time, Talent, & Resources

There are three gifts that we can contribute: time, talent, and resources. Everyone does not have the same amount of money and other resources. However, we all have the same amount of time: 168 hours in every week. If we multiply 168 hours by 10%, we have 16.8 hours. How many Christians give 16.8 hours per week to God's work? Do fathers and mothers give the full 168 hours because they are raising children who are made in the image of God? This is something that we must all address and seek the Holy Spirit's help for the answer to the time contribution question.

A Living Sacrifice

Perhaps the best way to handle the stewardship challenge is to present ourselves as a living sacrifice. In other words, when we give our body, mind, spirit, and soul to God, we have met all of the requirements of stewardship because we no longer own anything but have given everything to God. In Romans 12:1 (NIV), Paul stated:

Therefore, I urge you, brothers, in view of God's mercy, to offer your bodies as living sacrifices, holy and pleasing to God—this is your spiritual act of worship.

When we do this, we can be completely at peace about our stewardship responsibility because we have given everything that we have.

A Practical Way to Give

When the Corinthian church asked about collections, Paul addressed the issue in the following practical way:

On the first day of every week, each one of you should set aside a sum of money in keeping with his income, saving it up, so that when I come no collections will have to be made.[5]

Please notice that Paul does not state 10% or any other percentage. The amount is to be "in keeping with his income." This is a good practical way to determine the amount to be given.

In II Corinthians 9:6-7 (NIV), we see that God loves a giver with a good attitude. In that passage, it states:

[6]*Remember this: Whoever sows sparingly will also reap sparingly, and whoever sows generously will also reap generously.* [7]*Each man should give what he has decided in his heart to give, not reluctantly or under compulsion, for God loves a cheerful giver.*

As God owns everything in the universe, why would He want anything that we could give to Him? We are to give to show our love for God and for what He has already done for us.

Jesus Criticized Some Forms of Tithing

In fact, Jesus criticized some forms of tithing. In Matthew 23:23-24 (NIV), Jesus blasted the scribes and Pharisees for their perverted system of tithing:

> [23] *Woe to you, teachers of the law and Pharisees, you hypocrites! You give a tenth of your spices—mint, dill and cumin. But you have neglected the more important matters of the law—justice, mercy and faithfulness. You should have practiced the latter, without neglecting the former.* [24] *You blind guides! You strain out a gnat but swallow a camel.*

Wow! What a scathing indictment against the manipulation and perversion of inappropriate tithing. We are to give from an overflowing heart and not as a vain ritual to meet the letter of the law.

Make all that you can; give all that you can so that God may be glorified and magnified. Anything less than that may not be well received by God as the above passage indicates.

Too Much Giving?

Is it possible to give too much for the Lord's work? Please consider the following example. In Exodus 35:4-5 (NIV):

> [4] *Moses said to the whole Israelite community, "This is what the Lord has commanded:* [5] *From what you have, take an offering for the Lord. Everyone who is willing is to bring to the Lord an offering of gold, silver, and bronze;*

In verses 20-21 of that same passage, the following verses describe the reaction to Moses' admonition:

> [20] *Then the whole Israelite community withdrew from Moses' presence,* [21] *and everyone who* **was willing and whose heart moved him** *came and brought an offering to the Lord for the*

work on the Tent of the Meeting, for all its service, and for the sacred garments. [Emphasis added.]

There were a number of other items and skills presented for the work of the Lord. In Exodus 35:29 (NIV), Moses summarized the giving activity in the following way:

²⁹All the Israelite men and women who were willing brought to the Lord freewill offerings for all of the work the Lord through Moses had commanded them to do.

Finally, in Exodus 36:4-7 (NIV), the following announcement was made:

⁴So all the skilled craftsmen who were doing all the work on the sanctuary left their work ⁵and said to Moses, "The people are bringing more than enough for doing the work the Lord commanded to be done." ⁶Then Moses gave an order and they sent this word throughout the camp: "No man or woman is to make anything else as an offering for the sanctuary." And so people were restrained from bringing more, ⁷because what they already had was more than enough to do all of the work.

What caused the "whole Israelite community" to give more than was needed? Perhaps the answer to that question comes from the phrase, *who was willing and whose heart moved him.* When God touches a person's heart, there is no limit on the amount of giving that they are willing to make.

Chapter Summary

As we are under grace and not under the law, the New Testament criteria for giving is different from the legal requirement of the tithe (10%) in the Old Testament. Ten percent is a good starting point for contributions but not an upper boundary. Jesus highly commended the poor widow when she gave her mite because it was 100% of her means and all that she had to live on. Paul suggests that giving should be in keeping with our income.

CHAPTER 14

PROSPERITY, SUCCESS, MANAGEMENT &
OTHER TOPICS

"...For I know the plans I have for you," declares the Lord,
"plans to prosper you and not to harm you, plans to give you hope
and a future..." **Jeremiah 29:11 (NIV)**

The concluding chapter in this book is a potpourri of assorted topics dealing with financial matters and the fruit of good business and life decisions. It is designed to provide helps for a life lived to the fullest.

God's Plans for YOU

Jeremiah 29:11 (above) was given to the children of Israel when they were about to go into the 70 year captivity in Babylon. However, it has the same application to all believers today just as it did to the Jewish people then. God desires to prosper all of his children ultimately with a home in heaven. Many are going to prosper on this earth before they get to heaven. Some may have to endure some special training just as Job, David, Moses, Paul, and other saints have experienced before the prosperity arrives. All Christians can have a life of real joy regardless of their circumstances because they are on a road to God's heaven with a bright shining new mansion awaiting their arrival and all of the other benefits and joys associated with it.

Prosperity and Success

Virtually everyone desires prosperity and success according to the standards that they have set for those two qualities. Joshua 1:8 provides the formula for both *prosperity and success* from God's standards. Before we can utilize Joshua 1:8, we must apply II Timothy 2:15 (NET):

Make every effort to present yourself before God as a proven worker who does not need to be ashamed, teaching the message of truth accurately.

The sentence is in the imperative form with "you" understood as the subject. It commands that we need to have diligent effort to learn the Scriptures. One way to know the Scriptures is to memorize them. Psalm 119:11 states:

> In my heart I store up your words, so I might not sin against you.[1]

When we have studied and learned the Bible's message, then we are ready to apply Joshua 1:8:

> This book of the law must never be off your lips; you must keep it in mind day and night so that you may diligently observe everything that is written in it. Then you will prosper and be successful in everything you do.[2]

That is the formula for prosperity and success from God's point-of-view.

Ill-gotten Gains

No good comes from ill-gotten wealth; uprightness is a safeguard against death.[3] In a dark period of American commercial history, the captains of industry at Enron, WorldCom, Adelphia, HealthSouth, and other companies where ill-gotten gains were obtained, learned that honesty and integrity are very desirable characteristics. They also discovered quickly that dishonesty and fraud do not pay. Many of them have spent time in prison while Ken Lay of Enron died before his formal sentencing. While they were employed, they received very high remuneration. However, they enjoyed very little of their earnings after they were charged legally. It is truly sad that they did not apply the prohibition against ill-gotten wealth. Let us all learn from their mistakes.

Personnel Management—Boaz Style

In the little book of Ruth, Boaz stands out as a great role model for employee relations and management. In an age where there has been great animosity between employers and employees, we would do well to avoid the adversarial relationship that has characterized many industries in this century and the last. A good working relationship between management and workers might increase productivity and profits. When jobs are outsourced to other countries, members of the labor force lose in many instances and quality control may be diminished. In addition, the production process may become a more complicated system because of differences in cultures and other factors.

In the story of Ruth, Boaz showed spiritual concern for his workers; and they, in turn, had very warm relations with him. While Ruth was gleaning the field of Boaz, as was the custom for that day and time, the following exchange took place between Boaz and his workers:

> *Just then Boaz arrived from Bethlehem and greeted the harvesters, "The Lord be with you!" "The Lord bless you!" they called back.*[4]

Please notice that both quotations end with an exclamation point and emphasize some very strong feelings on both sides. Not all translations have an exclamation point for each quote but many do.

Owners, managers, and administrators need employees or they would not have hired them in the first place. On the other hand, workers need employment so that they can provide the basic necessities of life for themselves and their families.

The Christian Work Ethic and Taking Care of Business

In many instances, we would do well to take care of business and stay out of the limelight. Paul told the church at Thessalonica to practice that behavior. The New Century Version hits the essence of Paul's admonition:

> *Do all you can to live a peaceful life. Take care of your own business and do your own work as we have already told you. If you do, then people who are not believers will respect you and you will not have to depend on others for what you need.*[5]

In addition to living a peaceful life, there are two outcomes from the application of that text:

1. Non-believers will respect you. This may open up an opportunity for witnessing.
2. You will not depend on others. You will depend on the Lord instead.

Paul also covers the opposite of a good Christian work ethic. In his second letter to the Thessalonians, Paul states very forcefully the outcome of a poor work ethic:

"If a man will not work, he shall not eat." [6]

Obviously, the result in this case is not a good one.

Silver and Gold

In today's society, gold and silver are sought by many. However, the Bible promotes something other than silver and gold. In Proverbs 16:16, Solomon states:

How much better than gold it is to get wisdom, and to gain discernment is more desirable than silver. [7]

Silver and gold may be lost, stolen, or tarnished, but wisdom and discernment remain.

Contentment

Which is better, to have more resources without contentment or to have fewer resources with contentment? The writer of Hebrews says:

Do not live for money; be content with what you have... [8]

Proverbs declares:

The fear of the Lord leads to life: Then one rests content, untouched by trouble. [9]

It is clear that contentment is better than having more resources. In Paul's letter to Timothy, it is stated in this manner:

But godliness with contentment is great gain. For we brought nothing into this world and it is certain that we can carry nothing out.[10]

Actually, more assets may bring on more problems. Contentment is a state of mind that should be relished and enjoyed but it cannot be purchased. The Apostle Paul wrote to the church in Philippi and described his contentment as follows:

I know what it is to be in need, and I know what it is to have plenty. I have <u>learned</u> the secret to being content in any and every situation, whether well fed or hungry, whether living in plenty or want.[11] [Emphasis added.]

If the Apostle Paul **learned** to be content in all situations, perhaps we can as well. We would all be better off if we learned to enjoy the manifold blessings that the Lord has provided and not strive foolishly for more and more things.

<u>Conclusion</u>

It my prayer that this resource will help you become a better Christian, a better Christian witness and to enjoy life to the fullest. If you would like to discuss anything further, please contact me @ posey. bib.prin@gmail.com. May God bless you richly and cause His face to shine upon you.

ENDNOTES

King James Version Unless Otherwise Stated

Chapter 2

1. Exodus 22:25-27, 23:11, Leviticus 19:15, 25:25, 39, 47-48, Deuteronomy 24:12, and others
2. Deuteronomy 15:4-6
3. Ruth 2:1
4. Job 1:3 and Job 42:12
5. Matthew 27:57
6. Daniel 2:48
7. Luke 13:30
8. Psalm 1:3
9. Deuteronomy 29:9 (NIV)
10. Matthew 19:24, Mark 10:25, Luke 18:25
11. Deuteronomy 8:17-18 (NIV)

Chapter 3

1. Luke 14:28-30 (NASB)
2. Luke 14:31-32 (NASB)
3. Proverbs 31:16 (NIV)
4. Proverbs 29:18a (AMP)
5. James Strong, The Exhaustive Concordance of the Bible, Abingdon Press, New York, 1890, "Hebrew and Chaldee Dictionary," p. 38.
6. Proverbs 24:27 (RSB)
7. Proverbs 24:27 (LB)_
8. Proverbs 16:9 (NIV)
9. Proverbs 16:9 (REB)
10. James 4:13-15 (TM)

Chapter 4

1. I Thessalonians 4:11 (TM)
2. Psalm 37:23 (NASB)
3. Philippians 2:14 (NEB)
4. Colossians 3:22-25 (TM)
5. Ephesians 6:5-8 (NIV)

6. I Corinthians 10:31 (NIV)
7. Proverbs 28:19 (NIV)
8. Proverbs 23:4 (NASB)
9. Proverbs 15:19 (LB)
10. Proverbs 18:9 (NIV)
11. Proverbs 21:25 (REB)
12. Proverbs 20:13 (NIV)
13. Romans 12:10-11
14. Proverbs 13:11 (LB)
15. Proverbs 14:23 (LB)
16. Proverbs 13:19
17. Ephesians 5:16
18. Ecclesiastes 3:1-3, 8, 11a
19. Proverbs 12:24 (NEB)
20. Exodus 20:8-11 (NIV)
21. Genesis 37:2, 41:46
22. Psalm 37:23
23. Deuteronomy 24:5 (NIV)

Chapter 5

1. James 3:10 (NASB)
2. Julius Shakespeare, <u>Hamlet</u>, Act I, Scene III, Line 58, from <u>The Complete Works of Shakespeare</u>, Edited by Hardin Craig, (Scott, Foresman & Co., 1961), p. 909
3. Psalm 37:21 (REB)
4. Proverbs 22:7 (TM)
5. Matthew 5:42 (REB)
6. Luke 6:35 (NASB)
7. Psalm 112:5 (NIV)
8. Psalm 37:25-26 (NIV)
9. Deuteronomy 15:6 (NIV)
10. Exodus 22:25 (NIV)
11. Deuteronomy 23:19-20 (NASB)
12. Matthew 25:27 (NASB)
13. Proverbs 22:1 (NIV)
14. Ecclesiastes 7:1 (NIV)
15. I Timothy 6:8 (REB)
16. Philippians 4:19 (REB)

Chapter 6

1. Philippians 4:11 (NIV)
2. Hebrews 13:5 (NASB)
3. Psalm 17:15 (LB)
4. Haggai 1:6 (NIV)
5. Matthew 6:33 (RSV)
6. Matthew 13:45-46 (NIV)
7. Amos 8:4-6 (REB)
8. Proverbs 22:6 (NIV)
9. Daniel 6:14
10. Mark 6:22b-25 (NIV)
11. Proverbs 6:6-8 (REB)
12. Luke 15:14 (NIV)
13. Proverbs 20:14 (LB)
14. Proverbs 21:20 (LB)
15. Proverbs 21:20 (NEB)
16. Nehemiah 10:31 (NIV)
17. Proverbs 23:23 (NIV)
18. John 14:6 (NIV)

Chapter 7

1. Genesis, Chapters 6 & 7
2. Luke 2:7
3. Matthew 26:18
4. Matthew 8:20 (RSV)
5. Mark 6:10 (RSV)
6. John 14:2 (LB)
7. Revelation 21:21 (NIV)
8. Isaiah 11:6 (REB)
9. John 14:2-3
10. I Timothy 6:8 (NIV)
11. James 1:17 (NIV)
12. Psalm 127:1a (NIV)
13. Proverbs 17:1 (NIV)
14. John 14:13 (NIV)
15. Jeremiah 29:1, 4-5 (NIV)
16. Exodus 20:17a
17. Proverbs 12:7 (NIV)
18. Proverbs 22:7 (REB)

Chapter 8

1. Luke 18:18-25 (NIV), [Also found in Matthew 19:16-29 and Mark 10:17-30]
2. Luke 12:16-21 (NIV)
3. Matthew 6:19-21 (NIV)
4. Matthew 25:21
5. Matthew 25:27 (NIV)
6. Colossians 3:23 (NIV)
7. Luke 19:13b (NIV)
8. Luke 19:23 (NIV)
9. I Timothy 6:10 (NIV)
10. Genesis 12:1-3 (AMP)
11. Genesis 24:35 (NET)
12. Job 1:3 (AMP)
13. Job 2:7 (NIV)
14. Job 1:1 (NIV)
15. Job 42:1-2 (NIV)
16. Job 42:12 (NIV)
17. Job 42:15 (NIV)
18. Job 13:15
19. Job 19:25 (NIV)
20. Philippians 1:21
21. James 4:3 (NIV)

Chapter 9

1. Exodus 3:8
2. Genesis 13:14-15
3. Romans, Chapter 11
4. Galatians 3:28
5. II Samuel 3:12
6. Psalm 50:9-12 (NIV)
7. Acts 4:34-35a
8. I Chronicles 4:40 (NIV)
9. Genesis 11:1-4 (NIV)
10. Genesis 11:8-9 (NIV)
11. Matthew 23:12 (NIV)
12. Psalm 103:1-2
13. Leviticus 25:23 (AMP)

14. I Kings Chapter 21
15. Luke 20:46-47 (NIV)
16. Proverbs 10:2 (REB)
17. Proverbs 22:1 (NIV)

Chapter 10
1. Matthew 25:14, 15b (REB)
2. I Corinthians 10:25-31 (NLT)
3. Ecclesiastes 11:2 (REB)
4. Ecclesiastes 11:1
5. Proverbs 15:22 (NIV)

Chapter 11
1. Proverbs 15:22 (NLT)
2. Matthew 17:27 (NLT)

Chapter 12
1. Luke 10:27 (NCV)
2. Ecclesiastes 12:13 (NKJV)
3. Micah 6:8 (TCR)
4. Deuteronomy 10:12-13 (NIV)
5. Deuteronomy 11:26-27 (TCR)
6. Numbers 8:19 (NIV)
7. Numbers 8:23-26 (NIV)
8. Exodus 2:1-10
9. Exodus 2:12
10. Exodus 3:1-10
11. Deuteronomy 34:4 (NIV)
12. Acts 13:22 (NIV)
13. II Samuel 11:1-17
14. I Kings 1:1-2 (NIV)
15. Philippians 4:19
16. Philippians 4:6 (NIV)

Chapter 13

1. Mark 12:41-44 (NIV) and also given in Luke 21:1-4
2. Matthew 9:4 (NASB)
3. Psalm 50:10 & 12
4. Matthew 6:20

Chapter 14

1. Psalm 119:11 (NET)
2. Joshua 1:8 (REB)
3. Proverbs 10:2 (REB)
4. Ruth 2:4 (NIV)
5. I Thessalonians 4:11-12 (NCV)
6. II Thessalonians 3:10b (NIV)
7. Proverbs 16:16 (REB)
8. Hebrews 13:5 (REB)
9. Proverbs 19:23 (NIV)
10. I Timothy 6:6-7
11. Philippians 4:12 (NIV)